UPDATED EDITION

JOHN ELDREDGE

THE SACRED ROMANCE

WORKBOOK

COMING HOME
TO THE GOD WHO
PURSUES YOUR HEART

HarperChristian
Resources

The Sacred Romance Workbook (Updated Edition)
© 2000, 2024 by John Eldredge

Published in Grand Rapids, Michigan, by HarperChristian Resources. HarperChristian Resources is a registered trademark of HarperCollins Christian Publishing, Inc.

Requests for information should be sent to customercare@harpercollins.com.

ISBN 978-0-310-17213-0 (softcover)
ISBN 978-0-310-17214-7 (ebook)

All Scripture quotations, unless otherwise noted, are taken from the Holy Bible, New International Version®, NIV®. Copyright © 1973, 1978, 1984, 2011 by Biblica, Inc.® Used by permission. All rights reserved worldwide.

Scripture quotations noted NASB are from the New American Standard Bible®, Copyright © 1960, 1971, 1977, 1995, 2020 by The Lockman Foundation. All rights reserved.

Scripture quotations noted MSG are from The Message: The New Testament in Contemporary English. Copyright © 1993, 2002, 2018 by Eugene H. Peterson.

Scripture quotations noted NLT are from the Holy Bible, New Living Translation, copyright © 1996, 2004, 2015 by Tyndale House Foundation. Used by permission of Tyndale House Publishers, Inc., Carol Stream, Illinois 60189. All rights reserved.

Scripture quotations noted KJV are from The King James Version of the Bible.

HarperChristian Resources titles may be purchased in bulk for church, business, fundraising, or ministry use. For information, please e-mail ResourceSpecialist@ChurchSource.com.

Published in association with Yates & Yates (www.yates2.com).

First Printing October 2024 / Printed in the United States of America

CONTENTS

To all those who hear the Romance calling

INTRODUCTION

AN ADVENTURE BEGINS

Picture yourself in an ancient European city—Florence, perhaps, or Madrid. You find yourself at dusk, wandering through the older parts of town. Narrow streets are lined with dimly lit shops—pawnbrokers, no doubt, alongside various dealers in antiquities, booksellers, and curious haunts harboring mysteries from far-off lands.

Gas lamps flicker through sooty windows and open doorways. Partly out of curiosity, partly out of a wish to avoid the jostling crowds, you turn into a musty parlor. As your eyes adjust to the twilight inside, you discover aisles crammed with Babylonian trinkets, Persian rugs, suits of armor, Colombian pottery. You browse indifferently among the hanging baskets and leaning shelves crammed with everything old and intriguing.

Then something catches your eye. Sitting in a pile of forgotten silver urns and incense burners, it might have escaped your notice altogether. But it seemed to call to you, whisper your name. In fact, it is already in your hands. *This is ridiculous*, you think. You turn the lamp over and over most carefully, looking for . . . you're not quite sure what. Obviously it is from the Middle East; Arabia most likely. *What am I thinking? These things happen only in fairy tales.*

Something you read long ago—was it in Chesterton?—crosses your mind. "An adventure is, by its nature, a thing that comes to us. It is a thing that chooses us, not a thing that we choose."[1] *He's right about that,* you admit. *Alice wasn't looking for Wonderland when she fell through the looking-glass. Come to think of it, the four children just stumbled into Narnia through the back of the wardrobe. Anodos simply woke to find fairy-land had taken over his bedroom.*

But another voice rises within you, urging caution. *You've got places to go, for heaven's sake. Don't let yourself get carried away.* The voice is full of common sense, of course. It seems the very word of reason. But the voice also seems old and tired. From how many adventures has it swayed you in your life? How many dreams left in the closet? "Closing time," calls the curator of the shop. He begins to blow out the lamps. Your heart is racing. Somewhere back in your mind you hear the voice urging you on to your duties. But it is too late.

You've already rubbed the lamp.

CONGRATULATIONS! OR SHOULD I SAY, "BON VOYAGE"?

You must be looking for something since you picked up this workbook. There must be a thirst in you and a spirit just a little bit adventurous. For what you are holding in your hands is an invitation to a remarkable journey. No, it is more than that. It is a treasure map. And it will take you on the quest for the most beautiful and elusive of all treasures . . . your own heart and the heart of God. Like any true journey, it will hold surprises, dangers, mystery, romance, battle, and—as we always hope—a happy ending.

This is not for the fainthearted. It is for the lighthearted, the bravehearted, the brokenhearted, perhaps even the hard-hearted. But not for the half-hearted. (Unless, of course, you want the other half back. In which case you wouldn't really be halfhearted, would you?) Anyway, if you are looking for *more* out of your life . . .

more laughter
more intimacy
more beauty
more adventure
more of God

... then this workbook is for you. If you'd rather stay home and watch *Wheel of Fortune* reruns, you'd better put this down right now. I'm serious. Put the book down and back away slowly. You've got places to go, for heaven's sake. But my guess is, it's too late. All along you've been thinking that it's your choice, but you forget Chesterton. The adventure has chosen you.

HOW TO GET THE MOST OUT OF THIS WORKBOOK

This workbook is meant to be a companion to the updated edition of *The Sacred Romance—Drawing Closer to the Heart of God* by Brent Curtis and John Eldredge (Nelson Books, 2024). Reading *The Sacred Romance* has been for many people a deep and profound experience; "life-changing" is the nearly universal response. I am deeply grateful to report that the book has brought to many people a new freedom for their hearts, intimacy with God, and the story they've always been looking for.

The Sacred Romance Workbook is more than a study manual; it is a guided journey of the heart using exercises, journaling, and the arts. I suppose that the aim of most study guides is to help the reader better grasp the material at hand. But the goal of this workbook is to usher you into an *experience*. And that experience is the recovery of your heart and the discovery of your life as part of God's great Romance.

Let me explain how it works.

Each chapter in the workbook coincides with its parallel in *The Sacred Romance*. All quotes that are not otherwise attributed are taken from the corresponding chapter in the book. You will find it most helpful to use them together, employing the workbook *after* you've read the companion chapter in the book. Read the chapter first, before you approach the exercises in the workbook. You will benefit more by letting the book speak to you without "looking for the answers." This isn't a test, after all. No one is going to grade you on any of it.

WINDOWS

Many things that speak to our hearts are difficult to contain in a book but are necessary to the journey we are on. Movies, music, and art, for example. These are more than nice decorations or amusements. They are means of grace; gifts that we desperately need. They are quite often more powerful than mere proposition. I like Ken Gire's phrase: "Windows of the Soul."[2]

I've included with each chapter a selection of windows that I have found to be deeply helpful in my journey. Use them where and when you will. Of course, use the windows that you have come to know and love as well. You might find it helpful to begin each workbook session with a look through one of the windows, and then perhaps close your time with one. Some of the music I recommend is instrumental, such as the film scores. You might want to play one in the background as you read the chapter in *The Sacred Romance*. In whatever way you use the windows, by all means, use them.

THE JOURNAL

Space has been provided in this workbook for you to respond to the questions. But there are times when I will prompt you to write down your reflections in a journal to help you in your journey (journals are for *journeys;* diaries are merely for keeping track of the day's events; and personal organizers are . . . well, they rule your life). The exercises and windows will stir you, I hope. There won't be nearly enough space to catch all your thoughts and feelings and revelations in the workbook. And you may want to spend more time on a particular exercise. Some things are going to strike you—thoughts will come, out of the blue, and seem to have no bearing on the exercise at hand. So as you go along, capture those thoughts in your journal.

GROUPS

The Sacred Romance has been used with great success by study groups in churches, homes, businesses, and campus ministries. I've tried to design the workbook to serve both individuals and groups. Here are a few hints to group leaders:

- *Take advantage of the windows.* Use one or two of the suggested scenes and songs for your meeting. You may want to begin your time with a window. This is how I teach *The Sacred Romance*. I also typically close with one. (You'll want to use quality equipment, though. The power of the window is lost if the picture is fuzzy or the sound is harsh.)

- *Don't try to use your group time to complete the exercises.* Use it to talk about what your group members have discovered as they've done the exercises during the week. Your group time is a wonderful chance for them to process what they're learning. The exercises can be a great launching point for discussion.

- *Lead by example.* This is a very personal journey. Many people will find it hard to jump in and start sharing the deep places of their hearts and lives. I suggest you go first; don't dominate the time, but let your vulnerability create a safe place for theirs.

- *Warning:* You can't possibly cover in a group meeting all the material in the workbook. Two or three of the questions may be all you will have time to discuss, especially if you use some of the recommended film and music.

A WORD OF EXPLANATION

Brent Curtis and I wrote *The Sacred Romance* together. I wish we could have written this workbook together, but Brent was killed in a rock climbing accident in May 1998. I hate to tell readers in this way—I would rather sit down in person, tell you the whole story, listen to your questions, and tell you what God has done since that time. Some of that story is included in the book I wrote after Brent's death, *The Journey of Desire* (Nelson Books, 2016). Perhaps you will find it helpful. Many people miss Brent very much. Readers who never met him feel as though they know him as a close friend through the book. I hope you will as well. In fact, the story of *The Sacred Romance* will take on a much more profound meaning now that you know.

Not fare well,
But fare forward, voyagers.

T. S. ELIOT

1

THE LOST LIFE OF
THE HEART

Thirsty hearts [are those] whose longings have been wakened by the touch of God within them.

A. W. TOZER[3]

YOUR INITIAL REACTION

In two or three minutes, jot down the things that struck you when you read this chapter. What were your initial thoughts, emotions, impressions? (There's no need to edit your answers; don't try to make them sound "right" or "spiritual." One person told me after reading the chapter that he felt as though—finally—someone understood. But others have said they just didn't connect with the chapter at all. What was *your* response?)

I felt . . .

I realized . . .

I wanted . . .

I just didn't get this . . .

PRAYER OF BEGINNING

Search me, God, and know my heart (Psalm 139:23).

Dear Jesus, I ask you to come and lead me on this journey for my heart and for yours. Be my Guide, and help me to recover the lost life of my heart. When I am confused, grant me clarity and insight. When I am fearful and tempted to give up or check out, grant me courage to press on. When I am impatient or distracted, bring me back to what matters most. When I am hurting, comfort me. But in all, I pray you restore me to the fullness of the heart you set within me. In your name I pray. Amen.

TO CLARIFY

Here are the central truths of this chapter:

- We have an external life, which consumes most of us.
- We have an internal life, the life of the heart, which most of us have lost track of.
- The internal, the heart, is far more important; without it we cannot truly live or love or even know God.
- It is possible to recover the lost life of the heart—and very, very much worth the effort.

SOMETHING IS MISSING

The Sacred Romance begins by capturing an experience that many people have reported—a nagging awareness that things just aren't as they should be. We have within us a deep desire for the life we long to live . . . but something is missing. Our hearts cannot help but wonder, *Where are you, God, in all of this?* If we listen carefully, our hearts will tell us something priceless and promising: *This can't be it. There is something more.*

Do you have moments when you want more out of life? Take a few minutes now and write down the things you find yourself longing for, thirsting for, yearning for.

—— **LISTEN TO** ——
YOUR HEART

Brent writes of how our hearts are least edited in the still hours of the night. This can be the best time for hearing from your heart, without all the demands of the day. If you wake up in the middle of the night or find it hard to fall asleep, don't fight it. Listen. Use your journal to capture what you hear.

Was it difficult to come up with something to write about? Perhaps you do not find yourself "thirsty" at all. What might that say about how you handle your heart?

Let's approach it another way. On a scale of 1 to 10 (with 10 being the most enjoyment), how much are you enjoying your life right now? Is this more or less than you were, say, five years ago? Fifteen years ago?

How has your life turned out differently from the way you thought it would? What would you feel if you knew nothing would change in your situation for the rest of your life?

===================== **IF YOU ARE FEELING . . .** =====================

Sometimes Christians are uncomfortable admitting that they are not completely content with their lives. Many of us have been taught that a Christian is always, in the words of one camp song, "inright, outright, upright, downright happy all the time." So you might be feeling that these questions about heart and thirst are misguided. Consider what Christian psychologist Gerald May points out:

> In our society, we have come to believe that discomfort always means something is wrong. We are conditioned to believe that feelings of distress, pain, deprivation, yearning and longing mean something is wrong with the way we are living our lives. Conversely, we are convinced that a rightly lived life must give us serenity, completion and fulfillment. Comfort means "right" and distress means "wrong." The influence of such convictions is stifling to the human spirit. Individually and collectively, we must somehow recover the truth. The truth is, we were never meant to be completely satisfied.[4]

In fact, Augustine summed up "the whole life of the good Christian" as "a holy *longing*."[5] C. S. Lewis wrote that "when we consider the un-blushing promises of reward and the staggering nature of the rewards promised in the Gospels, it would seem that Our Lord finds our desires not too strong, but too weak."[6]

These deep yearnings of the heart—how often would you say you let them "speak" to you? Daily? Weekly? Monthly? Once or twice a year?

How do you typically respond to moments of yearning? Do you try to get past them? Feel embarrassed by them? Embrace them? Often, we simply bury them beneath busyness or appease our hearts with little indulgences such as food, a hobby, or another pleasure. Which option do you see as true for you?

WINDOW

But often, in the world's most crowded streets,
But often, in the din of strife,
There rises an unspeakable desire
After the knowledge of our buried life.

MATTHEW ARNOLD, "THE BURIED LIFE"[7]

THE EXTERNAL LIFE

In chapter 1, we point out a very important reality: We all live a double life. "On the outside, there is the external story of our lives. This is the life everyone sees, our life of work and play and church, of family and friends, paying bills, and growing older." According to the chapter, what are some of the qualities that typically make up our external lives?

"Our external story is where we carve out the identity most others know. It is the place where we have learned to label each other in a way that implies we have reached our final destination. Bob is an accountant; Mary works for the government; Ted is an attorney." How do you think others would label you from the outside?

Take five minutes and write down ten things you do in a typical week. Choose this past week, unless for some reason it was not typical (for example, you were on vacation). Include the activities of your spiritual life, but don't edit or choose the "better" or more important-sounding things. Simply write down as many activities as you can (for example, brush my teeth; file expense report; have a quiet time; take Jamie to soccer; make dinner; call New York account).

Now, look over your list. Put a check mark by the activities you did more out of duty or obligation (you felt you *ought* to have done them) and a plus sign by those you did more out of passion or desire (you *wanted* to do them). Sometimes it's a little of both. Did it feel *more* like duty or desire? When you have finished, do you have more checks or pluses?

WINDOW

In the film *Enchanted April,* Lottie and Rose are two proper, middle-class Englishwomen resigned to live weary lives and endure passionless marriages. One gray and gloomy winter day, in a long winter of gray and gloomy London days, Lottie sees an advertisement in the paper:

> *To those who love wisteria and sunshine. Small medieval Italian castle on the shores of the Mediterranean to be let furnished for the month of April. Servants included.*

She suggests the idea to Rose.

LOTTIE: Isn't it wonderful?

ROSE: Wonderful, yes . . . but it's not worth wasting one's time thinking about.

LOTTIE: Why don't we try and get it?

ROSE: Get it?

LOTTIE: Yes, not just say how wonderful it would be and then go back home to Hampstead, as we've been doing for years and years and years, without doing anything about it.

ROSE: But how do you mean, get it?

LOTTIE: Rent it, hire it, have it . . . the castle, the wisteria—everything. I'm sure it must be wrong to go on being good for so long you become miserable. I can see you've been good for years and years and you aren't happy. And I've been doing things for people ever since I was a little girl, and I don't believe I'm any better either.

As Brent mentions in this chapter, quite often what happens in the external life is that "busyness substitutes for meaning, efficiency substitutes for creativity, and functional relationships substitute for love." Where in your life are you experiencing a deep sense of meaning, as opposed to merely being busy?

And which of these activities allow you to live out your creativity, compared to simply trying to be efficient or productive?

And where do you experience love in all of it, which is different from making sure that your relationships are functioning, that everything is running smoothly?

When the external has taken over our lives, and we very seldom live from our heart, we end up living merely to survive. Has this ever happened to you? Is it happening now? What's it like?

THE INTERNAL LIFE

The other half of our "double life"—the inner life—is the story of our heart, "the life of the deep places within us—our passions and dreams, our fears and our deepest wounds." Most of us have a hard time defining what we mean by our *heart*. Jot down a few words that help you to understand *heart*. Perhaps you have only questions about heart right now. Write them down.

———————————————— **TO CLARIFY** ————————————————

Heart, as we use it in the book, means far more than emotions or feelings. In fact, our emotions are merely the outward expression of a deeper reality. They are like the indicator lights on a car's dashboard, letting you know what's going on "under the hood." Maybe it would help to ask yourself, "What have I been feeling lately? Angry? Tired? Joyful? Bored?" Now you know a bit more about how your heart is doing.

Look back at your answer about how others would label you from the outside. Do you feel that picture describes who you really are on the *inside*? If not, what's missing?

"The heart does not respond to principles and programs; it seeks not efficiency, but passion. Art, poetry, beauty, mystery, ecstasy: These are what rouse the heart. Indeed, they are the language that must be spoken if one wishes to communicate with the heart." Has anything moved you recently, stirred something inside you, bringing perhaps joy or tears? Take a moment to recall it now. Maybe a song reached you in such a way, a movie, or an event that happened to you or someone you love. It may be something as simple as a sunrise. Write a few words about why it stirred you, what you desired.

—— **LISTEN TO** ——
YOUR HEART

If you can, you might want
to return to the thing that
stirred your heart—the movie
or song or place. Listen again,
only more attentively.
Use your journal to capture
those stirrings.

There seems to be something similar in the yearnings of every human heart. Brent calls it "a yearning for intimacy, beauty, and adventure." For life as it was meant to be. Does that seem true of the things that have stirred your heart? For example, think about your favorite movies. Do they contain those themes?

THE *LOST* LIFE OF THE HEART

This chapter makes an assumption. We take it for granted that, given the way life unfolds for most of us, we have lost heart along the way.

WINDOW

"Along the Road" is a beautiful song written by Dan Fogelberg; I love the version sung by Margaret Becker. The chorus goes like this:

Joy at the start
Fear in the journey
Joy in the coming home
A part of the heart
Gets lost in the learning
Somewhere along the road.

Would you say your heart is free? On a scale of 1 to 10 (with 10 being the most free), how free? Why did you choose the number you did?

Let's explore that answer a bit. Speaking of our heart, Frederick Buechner says, "All real art comes from that deepest self—painting, writing, music, dance. . . . Our truest prayers come from there, too. . . . And I think that from there also come our best dreams and our times of gladdest playing."[8] Are you a more creative person now than you were in your youth? Do you paint? Write poetry? Play an instrument? Dance? If so, is it more or less than you used to? If not, if those things have no place in your life, why not? Do they seem frivolous to you?

When was the last time you "played," just had fun with carefree abandon? And before that, how long had it been?

What are your dreams for your life now? Does dreaming come naturally for you? Write down five dreams you currently hold for yourself.

=== **IF YOU ARE FEELING . . .** ===

All these questions are ways of exploring how much we may have "lost heart." Do you feel good about your answers? Is there something about the questions themselves that irritates you? "What's all this about dreams and dancing and playing?" some people have asked. "Shouldn't we just focus on the Lord, get on with serving him?" As we mention in chapter 1, we are *told* in Scripture to watch over our hearts with deep and sincere concern, for from our hearts flow "the springs of life" (Proverbs 4:23 NASB). Where there is no life, we have lost heart.

THE SPIRITUAL LIFE

Does your spiritual life currently seem to offer anything relevant to those deep yearnings of your heart? Or does it seem more like problems to be solved and principles to be mastered?

And what about the things that have most deeply stirred your heart—the songs and movies and sunrises and all? Do they come through the activities of church and Bible study, or do those stirrings more often come through other places in your life, such as your hobbies or your adventures?

In chapter 1, we define the Christian life as "a love affair of the heart, an adventure of epic proportion." How would you have defined the Christian life before reading this chapter? "The Christian life is . . ."

To the best of your understanding, how would your church answer this question? "The Christian life is . . ."

WINDOW

The psalms were given to us, among other things, to describe the inner life of those who know God. Here is how David describes his spiritual experience:

> *You, God, are my God,*
> *earnestly I seek you;*
> *I thirst for you,*
> *my whole being longs for you. . . .*
> *I sing in the shadow of your wings.*
> *I cling to you;*
> *your right hand upholds me.*

PSALM 63:1, 7–8

This sort of inner communion and thirst for God is not limited to biblical characters. Madame Guyon, for example, was a beautiful Frenchwoman of high society who came to Christ in 1668. Here is how she experienced God:

> Nothing was more easy to me now than to practice prayer. Hours passed away like moments, while I could hardly do anything else but pray. The fervency of my love allowed me no intermission . . . the taste of God was so great, so pure, so unblended and uninterrupted, that it drew and absorbed the powers of the soul . . . I love God far more than the most affectionate lover among men loves the object of his earthly attachment.[9]

How do you respond to David and Madame Guyon? What is it like to read their words? (Sometimes I feel like, *Yes, that's what I want.* Other times I feel more like, *What are they even talking about? I am a million miles from there.*)

Would you say that your spiritual life is more like theirs or, as Brent describes, has "communion with God [been] replaced by activity for God"?

Was there a time in your life when your experience of God seemed more intimate, when it addressed the core longings of your soul? Sometimes this is especially true of "first love" encounters, when a person comes to know God for the first time in his life. If you can recall such a time, or if you are enjoying one now, write a few words to describe it. You might even try your hand at a poem or a song.

If all that seems far away, then write about what you would like to experience with God.

WINDOW

Pete Docter, director of the animated film *Up,* conceived of the story based on fantasies of escaping from everyday life and a longing for something more. The plot centers on Carl Fredricksen, a balloon sales-man, who from a young age dreams of being an explorer. Carl promises his wife, Ellie, that they will take a trip to Paradise Falls, but they end up spending the money on more pressing needs. Ultimately, Ellie falls ill and dies before they can go on the journey. Now in his 70s, Carl determines to keep his promise by attaching thousands of balloons to fly his house to Paradise Falls. It's a great story of not only pursuing dreams but also the power of friendship and what truly matters in life.

We know from the Gospels that much of the Jewish religion was reduced to ritual by the time of Christ. Seeing that people's hearts had been hardened through religious duty, Jesus lamented, "These people honor me with their lips [ritual and rules], but their hearts are far from me" (Matthew 15:8).

At one point, Jesus went to Jerusalem for the Feast of Tabernacles. Tabernacles was a seven-day festival held at the end of the harvest season. It involved a great deal of religious sacrifice and ritual. "On the last day, the climax of the festival, Jesus stood and shouted to the crowds, 'Anyone who is thirsty may come to me! Anyone who believes in me may come and drink!'" (John 7:37–38 NLT).

Why do you think Jesus appealed to people's thirst to draw them to himself? Does it strike you as significant that he waited until the last day of the ritual to speak to their thirst? Why might that have been necessary?

———————————— **IF YOU ARE FEELING . . .** ————————————

Expressions such as "having a relationship with God" and "becoming a Christian" might be new to you, so let me explain. Christians believe that God is a person, and that we have personality because he does. Our hearts—with all their yearnings—are expressions of his. We believe that a relationship with God is not only possible but can also be the most intimate and satisfying love we'll ever know. Jesus of Nazareth claimed to be "God in the flesh," the eternal God come down to make himself known to mankind. When he offers to slake your thirst, he means he will come and satisfy your heart's deepest longings. "Coming to him" means believing in him, trusting him with your well-being now and forever.

The Sacred Romance can take you into an intimate relationship with God. All it requires is an open heart. You might begin your journey with a simple prayer such as this:

Jesus, I long to know you. Come to me. Reveal yourself to my heart.

How might God be drawing you through your thirst even now?

THE JOURNEY

"It is possible to recover the lost life of our heart and with it the intimacy, beauty, and adventure of life with God. To do so, we must leave what is familiar and comfortable—perhaps even parts of the religion in which we have come to trust—and take a journey." How do you feel about taking this journey? What are you hoping to find?

WINDOW

O God, I have tasted Thy goodness, and it has both satisfied me and made me thirsty for more. I am painfully conscious of my need of further grace. O God, the triune God, I want to want Thee; I long to be filled with longing; I thirst to be made more thirsty still. Begin in mercy a new work of love within me. Say to my soul, "Rise up my love, my fair one, and come away." Then give me grace to rise and follow Thee up from this misty lowland where I have wandered so long. In Jesus' name. Amen.

A. W. TOZER, *THE PURSUIT OF GOD*

WINDOWS

Film

Up (Walt Disney Studios Motion Pictures, 2009).

Enchanted April (Miramax Films, 1992). A truly wonderful British movie, which captures so well our longing for something more, for a better life. Set in England and Italy after World War I, the film centers on the lives of four women and three men whose lives change forever when they rent a villa on the Italian Riviera.

Music

I love film scores. They are written with a story in mind and seem to speak straight to my heart. I will recommend many as we go along.

Out of Africa motion picture soundtrack (MCA Records, 1985). Especially tracks 1 and 12. Also, "Along the Road," the title track from *Along the Road* by Susan Ashton, Margaret Becker, and Christine Dente (Sparrow Records, 1994).

Books

The Journey of Desire by John Eldredge (Nashville, TN: Nelson Books, 2016). This is in many ways the follow-on book to *The Sacred Romance*, which will help you to explore the journey of your heart through your deep desires.

The Pursuit of God by A. W. Tozer (Reynoldsburg, OH: Christian Publications, 1982). This is a short but deeply profound book.

2

AN UNKNOWN ROMANCING

We wake, if ever we wake at all, to mystery.

ANNIE DILLARD[10]

YOUR INITIAL REACTION

In two or three minutes, jot down the things that struck you when you read this chapter. What were your initial thoughts, emotions, impressions? (There's no need to edit your answers; don't try to make them sound "right" or "spiritual.")

I felt . . .

I realized . . .

I wanted . . .

I just didn't get this . . .

PRAYER OF BEGINNING

I remember the days of long ago (Psalm 143:5).

Dear Jesus, help me to recover my heart. Help me to recall the moments in my life when I felt most alive. Bring to mind memories long forgotten. Reveal to me how you have been calling to my heart, though I may never have seen it as your calling. In your name I pray. Amen.

TO CLARIFY

Here are the central truths of this chapter:

* There was a time when most of us felt wonder, knew we were made for a great romantic adventure.
* Those moments of longing as children reveal to us the deep heart set within us.
* And those moments of wonder and those deep longings are the way in which God has been wooing us.
* For this is the destiny for which we were created . . . a Sacred Romance.

"LISTEN TO YOUR LIFE"

The chapter begins with an invitation to "listen to our lives," to go back into our own stories and recover something precious that has been lost. As Frederick Buechner said, "If we keep our hearts and minds open as well as our ears, if we listen with patience and hope, *if we remember at all deeply and honestly*," then we may come to discover something about our true heart and the ways in which God has been calling to us.[11] Is this a new thought to you that to find God, you must find your own heart, listen to the story of your life? Are you eager or apprehensive to look back?

══════ IF YOU ARE FEELING . . . ══════

Many Christians have been told to forget the past; we should focus not on ourselves but on Christ and "press ahead." Advocates of this view point to Paul's letter to the Philippians (see 3:13–14). And yet Paul often spoke of his past; wrote fondly of friends and events from days gone by; and in 2 Timothy he urged his young disciple not to forget his youth, the legacy of faith he received from his grandmother and mother (see 1:5). In fact, the Scriptures are full of commands to remember the past and warnings of what happens when we forget the journey that God has brought us through. "Remember how the Lord your God led you" is a common theme.

Down through the ages, followers of Christ have found it not only helpful but also necessary to search out their own hearts in order to find God. *The Imitation of Christ* was written by a devout Dutch priest named Thomas à Kempis, who lived in the 1400s. It has been called the best-loved, most widely read religious book in the world, after the Bible. Many have found through it a deeper experience of God. So it might come as a surprise that à Kempis began by saying, "An humble knowledge of thyself is a surer way to God than a search after learning."

So, too, the famous Reformer John Calvin began his *Institutes of the Christian Religion,* written in the 1530s, with this statement: "True and substantial wisdom principally consists of two parts: the knowledge of God and the knowledge of ourselves."

EARLY RECOLLECTIONS OF ROMANCE

As you read Brent's story about his childhood on the farm, the cornfields and moonlight and streamside singers, the cowboy stories with bad guys and a pretty girl, what did it stir in you?

Recall one of your best memories from childhood: a Christmas with your grandparents perhaps, a family vacation, or a summer afternoon with a best friend. Tell your story as Brent told his, trying to recapture the sights and sounds, the aromas, the way it made you feel. (You'll want to use your journal for this one, to allow a bit more room).

Now linger over what you've recalled. Why is it a favorite memory? What did it offer your heart?

═══ WINDOW ═══

The movie *October Sky*—based on a true story—tells how one boy rises above enormous obstacles to pursue his dream of becoming a scientist. His only chance to go to college is winning the high school science contest by designing a model rocket that really flies. His buddy asks him, "What are the chances of us winning that science fair?" "A million to one," he replies. "That good? Well, why didn't you say so?" The rocket soars . . . and his dreams come true.

IF YOU ARE FEELING . . .

Our memories from the past will always be mixed. Brent warns that not only has "something wonderful wooed us" but that "something fearful has stalked us" as well. In this chapter, we focus on the Romance. Chapter 3 will give space for the memories that are not so glad.

However, you may be hard-pressed to recall happy images from your childhood. There are childhoods that have been so bleak as to seem only tragic. Then you must do as George MacDonald urged: "You must interpret the word by all that you have missed in life."[12] What you have not known but *wish* you had—let that be your teacher.

What were some of your favorite stories as a child? Books, movies, TV shows? A fairy tale perhaps, such as the Chronicles of Narnia? (My wife loved *A Little Princess*; I loved *The Wind in the Willows*.) What was it about those stories that you loved? Did you see yourself as one of the characters?

LISTEN TO YOUR HEART

You might want to go back and recover that story even now; read it or watch it again. What is it like to experience it as an adult? Journal about that.

Did you have a favorite object as a child—a toy or a pet perhaps? Why did you love it so?

Think about your favorite games as a child. What roles did you play? What did you long to be? Someone's hero? Someone's beauty?

TO CLARIFY

The word *romance* has been cheapened in our times. Many people associate it with dime-store novels or soap operas, with something syrupy and shallow. We will have much more to say about this as you read on, but for now let me attempt a definition of our use of the word. By *romance*, we mean a love story set in the midst of a life-and-death struggle; a great adventure, strewn with real dangers, with mystery around every corner. A drama that requires something heroic of us, where we are in the company of fellow travelers whose hearts we trust and whose hands we hold.

Brent says that the story all children naturally long for is one that involves intimacy and adventure, a story that invites us to be in "a relationship of heroic proportions." Do you see that to be true about the stories you loved as a child and the games you played?

"When I was a boy," wrote Brent, "I loved to jump from our haymow onto the backs of steers feeding at the hayrack directly underneath. The ensuing bareback ride was always an adventure of the highest order." Most children love adventure. "Firsts" are often unforgettable adventures. I'll never forget learning to ride a bike or the first time I galloped on horseback. What are some of the adventures you remember from your youth?

Did you ever do anything a little bit crazy? (I almost set the house on fire when I was six.)

And what are some of your favorite memories of intimacy as a child? Who were the special people in your life? Who were your best friends growing up?

WINDOW

In her song "Life Is Beautiful" (not to be confused with the motion picture of the same name), Michelle Tumes sings about her childhood and the dreams she had as a little girl:

She had no rings on her fingers
She had diamonds in her eyes
She had no money to be reckoned with
She had love within her life

And I heard her singing
Wouldn't you say
Wouldn't you say
Wouldn't you say that life is beautiful?

Brent recalls, "Watching television in the evenings, I would find a part of my boyish heart 'awakened' by a beautiful young girl onscreen when I felt that our eyes met." Do you recall your first infatuation? Your early experiences of romance?

"Remembering these scenes from my own story," said Brent, "I realized that I had found part of the lost journey of my heart." Sure, they may seem silly now, perhaps a bit embarrassing. But do you see something of your own heart in those memories?

"Each of us has a geography where the Romance first spoke to us. It is usually the place we both long to see again and fear returning to for fear our memories will be stolen from us." Do you have a place from your youth that you have longed to return to? Have you returned? Why or why not?

WINDOW

There is a reason Jesus said that "unless you change and become like little children, you will never enter the kingdom of heaven" (Matthew 18:3). Children, of all people, are able to live from the heart. They are still open to wonder.

> Up, heart, and sing.
> All things were made for us—we are God's heirs—
> Moon, sun, and wildest comets that do trail
> A crowd of small worlds for a swiftness-tail!
> Up from thy depths in me, my child-heart bring—
> The child alone inherits anything.

GEORGE MACDONALD, *DIARY OF AN OLD SOUL*[13]

THE ROMANCE NOW

And how about now? Are you catching glimpses of the Romance in your life as an adult? Brent spoke of finding it in "the golden fall of the Rockies and in the windswept sea grasses and whitecaps of bay and ocean on the Atlantic; in a quiet moment of sunlight orchestrated into parallel rays of warmth on my shoulder as I read a good book; in the eyes of certain women and the strength of certain men . . . at a movie when two lovers we know are meant to be together finally find each other—or don't." Take a few moments to write down several ways you've encountered the Romance recently.

Was it difficult to find any? If so, why might that be?

Think for a moment about how you spend your free time (or how you'd *like* to spend your free time if you had any). Lewis said that even in our hobbies, we are looking for the Romance.[14] Is it travel? Gardening? Sports? What makes it so enjoyable? Why does it make you come alive?

——— LISTEN TO ——— YOUR HEART

How might you cultivate the Romance in your life today? Are there places you can go on a regular basis, music you can return to, films you might want to watch again?

"Thankfully," wrote Brent, "our heart will not totally give up on the Romance." How are you longing for it today? Set your pen down for a moment and consider: *If you could do the very thing you secretly want to do, with no restraints whatsoever, what would you do?*

Dare you even write it down? Can you see the longing for intimacy and adventure in your answer?

MAKING THE VITAL CONNECTION

"Sadly, many of us never come to see this wooing, in whatever geography it first finds us, as having anything to do with our heart's deepest desire, our spiritual life, or our soul's destiny." The longings, the memories and what they stir, the childhood dreams, the way we are haunted by our secret desires—what do you suppose these have to do with Christianity?

=== **WINDOW** ===

The movie *Hidden Figures*, also based on a true story, is another powerful story about overcoming enormous obstacles to pursue one's longings and dreams. The story follows three African American women who work at NASA during the height of segregation in the 1960s. One of these women, Mary Jackson, works in the computing section but longs for something more: to be a NASA engineer. However, when she applies for the position, she is told it requires college courses that are only available locally at an all-white high school. Undeterred, she pleads her case in court, and the following scene unfolds:

JUDGE: Hampton High School is a white school, Mrs. Jackson.

MARY: Yes, your honor. I'm aware of that.

JUDGE: Virginia is still a segregated state. . . .

MARY: Your honor, you of all people should understand the importance of being first.

JUDGE: How's that, Mrs. Jackson?

MARY: Well, you were the first in your family to serve in the armed forces. U.S. Navy. The first to attend University. George Mason. . . .

JUDGE: What's the point here? . . .

MARY: I plan on being an engineer at NASA. But I can't do that without taking those classes at that all-white high school. And I can't change the color of my skin. So, I have no choice but to be the first, which I can't do without you. [She looks around the courtroom.] Your honor, out of all the cases you'll hear today, which one will matter in a hundred years? Which one will make you the "first"?

JUDGE: [Looks around the courtroom.] Only the night classes.

"Someone or something has romanced us from the beginning." This is the surprising message of chapter 2—that God is the One behind all the things that have ever moved our hearts. We know, for example, that the world of "creek-side singers and pastel sunsets . . . the austere majesty of snowcapped mountains and the poignant flames of autumn colors" has all been given to us to draw our hearts to God.

> *The heavens declare the glory of God;*
> *the skies proclaim the work of his hands.*
> *Day after day they pour forth speech;*
> *night after night they reveal knowledge.*
> *They have no speech, they use no words;*
> *no sound is heard from them* (Psalm 19:1–3).

And not just the created world, but the chapters of our own lives have been written by the One who is wooing us.

> *My frame was not hidden from you*
> *when I was made in the secret place,*
> *when I was woven together in the depths of the earth.*
> *Your eyes saw my unformed body;*
> *all the days ordained for me were written in your book*
> *before one of them came to be* (Psalm 139:15–16).

Through all this and more, God says, "I have loved you with an everlasting love; I have drawn you with unfailing kindness" (Jeremiah 31:3). How does that thought make you feel?

What does it do for your heart to consider that your deepest desires reveal what you were made for? And can you see something of God's wooing now as you look back over your life?

"The Romance comes and goes as it wills. And so we are haunted by it. . . . There are enough hints and clues and 'tantalizing glimpses' to keep us searching, our heart ever open and alive to the quest." Would you say that is true for you—that your heart is open and alive to the quest? Would you like it to be true?

WINDOW

Lord, teach me to listen. The times are noisy and my ears are weary with the thousand raucous sounds which continuously assault them. Give me the spirit of the boy Samuel when he said to Thee, "Speak, for thy servant heareth." Let me hear Thee speaking in my heart. Let me get used to the sound of Thy voice. Amen.

A. W. TOZER, *THE PURSUIT OF GOD*

WINDOWS

Film

October Sky (Universal, 1999).

Hidden Figures (20th Century Fox, 2016).

Music

When it comes to personal recollections, there is no substitute for the music we loved when we were young. Nearly everyone has personal taste in music. Quite often, it is the music we were listening to in our high school and college years (when we were still searching for the Romance). One friend calls it "the soundtrack of our lives." If it has been a while since you've listened to those old favorites, you might find them helpful in this part of the journey.

Life Is Beautiful motion picture soundtrack (Virgin Records, 1998). Especially tracks 1, 5, and 18.

"Life Is Beautiful" by Michelle Tumes, from *Listen* (Sparrow Records, 1998), track 10.

Photo Albums

Take a personal journey to your past by spending an evening looking at photos from your youth. Keep your journal nearby. For a really powerful experience, try listening to one of the movie soundtracks as background music.

Places

You may live within driving distance of the places that were special to you as a child. If so, you may want to visit them again. (Take your journal with you— you never know what will be stirred.)

Books

The Sacred Journey by Frederick Buechner (New York: HarperCollins, 1982). Buechner wrote his autobiography in three small journals. This was part one, *A Memoir of Early Days,* of the trilogy. The other two are also quite enjoyable—*Now and Then* and *Telling Secrets.*

Surprised by Joy by C. S. Lewis (New York: Harcourt Brace Jovanovich, 1955). His autobiography, subtitled *The Shape of My Early Life*.

The Awakened Heart by Gerald May (New York: HarperCollins, 1991).

3

THE MESSAGE OF
THE ARROWS

I wept when I was born, and every day shows why.

GEORGE HERBERT[15]

YOUR INITIAL REACTION

In two or three minutes, jot down the things that struck you when you read this chapter. What were your initial thoughts, emotions, impressions?

I felt . . .

I realized . . .

I wanted . . .

PRAYER OF BEGINNING

But you, Sovereign LORD,
  help me for your name's sake;
  out of the goodness of your love, deliver me.
For I am poor and needy,
  and my heart is wounded within me. . . .
Help me, LORD my God;
  save me according to your unfailing love (Psalm 109:21-22, 26).

Dear Jesus, it is true. Somewhere deep inside, my heart is wounded within me. I fear to even open up these places, and yet I long to be free, to know my heart is well. So come, take me by the hand, and lead me into the Arrows of my heart. Only do not leave me there, but lead me through to the fields of gladness and joy. In your name I pray. Amen.

TO CLARIFY

Here are the central truths of this chapter:

- There are only two things that pierce our heart—beauty and affliction.
- We have all known plenty of affliction.
- That affliction—what we call Arrows—brought with it a *message.*
- Until we deal with the Arrows and their messages, they will keep us from fully embracing the Romance and living as we were meant to live.

FACING YOUR ARROWS

Brent ended our discussion of the Romance by noting, "If this poignant longing were the only deep experience of our soul, then we should not lose heart. . . . But there is another message that comes to all of us in varying shades and intensities, even in our early years. It often seems to come out of nowhere and for no discernible reason that we can fathom. It is dark, powerful, and full of dread. I think of it as the Message of the Arrows."

In this chapter we face the other "voice," the other half of life's experience. We must stop and take time to thoughtfully, honestly, and tenderly answer these questions: "Think of how you've handled the affliction that has pierced your own heart. How did the Arrows come to you? Where did they land? Are they still there? What have you done as a result?"

How do you feel about going where these questions lead?

IF YOU ARE FEELING . . .

This may be the hardest chapter in the book for you to deal with. It certainly was the hardest chapter to write. We don't face our heart-breaks easily. Something deep in us, something almost instinctive, recoils at pain. Who in his right mind would volunteer for a root canal? But, as Brent said, "becoming a follower of Jesus doesn't necessarily solve the dilemma of the Arrows. . . . Mine were still lodged deep and refused to allow some angry wound inside to heal." To allow our hearts to heal, we must face our Arrows.

"If we deny the wounds or try to minimize them, we deny a part of our heart and end up living a shallow optimism that frequently becomes a demand that the world be better than it is. On the other hand, if we embrace the Arrows as the final word on life, we despair, which is another way to lose heart. To lose hope has the same effect on our heart as it would be to stop breathing. If only there were someone to help us reconcile our deepest longings with our greatest fears."

You can move forward in hope that there *is* Someone who can help. In Isaiah 61, the ministry of the Messiah is foretold. Why will Jesus come? What will he do? "He has sent me to bind up the brokenhearted . . . to comfort all who mourn" (verses 1–2). The comfort God offers comes only to those who mourn. But the comfort does come. So hang in there. This can be hard work, but it's worth it. Really.

ARROWS FROM OUR YOUTH

Most of the defining Arrows of our lives strike when we are young. For it is then that our hearts are most vulnerable and we are least guarded, least able to deal with the pain. Take some time now, with your journal, to write down a word or a sentence that captures for you the significant Arrows from your youth.

As Psalm 51:6 reminds us, God desires truth in the "innermost being" (NASB) in our *hearts*. We must be honest with ourselves about the heartaches of life. Because many of us have dealt with our pain by pushing it away, out of our conscious living, you may find it hard to recall the Arrows that you've known. Perhaps this prayer would be a good place to begin:

Dear Jesus, you desire truth in my inmost being, so I ask you to help me to be honest with myself about the Arrows of my life. Help me to remember. "Search me, O God, and know my heart." Reveal to me now the Arrows that remain deep in my soul. Let nothing remain hidden. And grant me the courage to face what you reveal. Amen.

——— **LISTEN TO** ———
YOUR HEART

Don't edit yourself; don't
stop to assess whether the
Arrows are "legitimate" or
worthy to be called Arrows.
You know what hurt you.
That's enough for now.

Write down a word or a sentence that captures for you the significant Arrows from your youth. For example:

Mother's cancer
Debbie
Missing the basket every time
Fatty
My parents' divorce

WINDOW

Some of you will have no problem with this. You know exactly what your Arrows are. Others will find it hard. You may want to use the windows to help you find those places in your heart. Many of the windows will be the same as they were for chapter 2—personal things such as old photos, places from the past, the music of your life. It might help you to recall the seasons of your life—youth (the early years), adolescence, high school.

I've suggested two films—*Shadowlands* and *A River Runs Through It*—because they capture well the innocence of youth and the impact of the Arrows. When I first saw *A River Runs Through It*, the film absolutely undid me; the story closely paralleled my own. I went to the theater to just enjoy a movie, and by the end, I was weeping. If that has happened to you—if a film brought you to tears in a personal way—it might be good to watch that film again. Keep your journal at hand. And a box of tissues.

THE MESSAGE

After you've recorded as many Arrows as have come to mind in this first round, stop to look over your list. What was the *message* of each Arrow? You see, it's not so much the pain you've experienced but *what you've learned* from it. After a broken engagement, one woman came to realize that the message she'd received was, "You will never be pursued; you will never truly be wanted." One man said that when his father divorced his mother, the message he heard as a boy was, "You're just not worth fighting for." Ask God to reveal to you the *message* of each Arrow.

> *Heavenly Father, you know all mysteries, and you can reveal what is hidden in the darkness. Show me the messages of each of these Arrows. Open the eyes of my heart to see the lessons that I learned. Help me put words to the messages. Amen.*

WINDOW

The movie *Shadowlands* tells how C. S. Lewis lost his wife, Joy, to cancer. Weeks, perhaps months, later, he is sitting in his study, the shock wearing off and the grief searing his soul. He says to his brother, Warnie, "Reality is a brutal teacher. But you learn . . . my God, you learn."

The question is, *What* do we learn?

Next to each of the words or sentences that you've written to record your Arrows, write down what you believe the message to have been. What did the Arrow say about you? About God? About others? About life in general? For example:

Mother's cancer = *God isn't good; he can't be trusted.*
Debbie = *I will never be loved.*
Missing the basket every time = *I don't belong . . . and never will.*
Fatty = *I am unlovely or unlovable.*
My parents' divorce = *No one will ever be there for me.*

Quite often the Arrows strike in the same place. Or at least, we interpret their messages as saying the same thing about us. Look over the messages you've written. Do you see a *theme* emerging? Is there a persistent message?

Can you hear those messages still playing in your life today?

HOW WE RESPOND

Brent said there are basically two ways we handle our Arrows. The first option is just to deaden our heart. *"If I don't want so much,* we believe, *I won't be so vulnerable. Instead of dealing with the Arrows, we silence the longing."* Think about the dreams you had when you were young. How does your life now compare to the dream? Do you begin to see why? You may be able to draw connections between a particular Arrow, its message, and the loss of heart you have experienced.

"There was a girl I loved," wrote Brent, "but couldn't love (intimacy requires a heart that is released and mine was pinned down with unknown fears and grief) and so I let her go." Are you comfortable with intimacy? How many close friends do you have in your life now? If you are married, is your marriage intimate on a heart-to-heart level? If you are not married, would you like to be? Is there something in the way?

Look at the exercises from chapter 1, where I asked you about the freedom of heart you have today. Is it possible that your answers to those questions are tied to your Arrows recorded here? For example, I asked about how much creativity is in your life. One woman realized that many years ago, she gave up her life's love—dancing—because she was supposed to be productive and efficient as an adult, and no one valued her as a dancer. Are there things lost in your past because you took an Arrow?

The second way we deal with our Arrows is to divide life into two parts. On the outside, all is duty and survival. But in secret, we find something to give us a taste of the intimacy and adventure we were made for. Are you plagued by an annoying habit? Are you dealing with an addiction that you can't control? Look back over the Arrows and the messages. Can you see a correlation? (For example, a young girl is taunted about her weight all through grade school. In college, she develops an eating disorder called anorexia, through which she guarantees herself a slender figure.)

Where do you go for a taste of intimacy or a taste of adventure these days?

THE VOW

We are all quite human, and our Arrows have hurt us very much. So we respond; we react. Brent wrote, "Our deepest convictions are formed without conscious effort, but the effect is a shift deep in our soul. Commitments form never to be in that position again, never to know that sort of pain again. The result is an approach to life that we often call our personality." Even though we may no longer feel the pain of our Arrows, they are shaping us still. The commitments Brent refers to are the deep resolutions we make in our hearts to live a certain way, forevermore. They really are something like vows. For example . . .

A little boy wants to play on the team. But at the first practice, he fails to hit the ball, and his teammates mock him mercilessly. He vows, *I will never try that again.* And for the rest of his life, he never plays sports. He says he prefers to read by himself.

A little girl watches her mother, an alcoholic, drink herself to death. She vows, *I will never, ever do anything bad in all my life.* She becomes a moral perfectionist and is rewarded for her Christian "faith."

Can you remember making a vow after a painful Arrow struck? What did you resolve to do—or never do—again?

Perhaps you can't remember a time and place you made an actual vow. But can you see how your Arrows—and their messages—shaped the way you approach life? Think about the way you relate to others. Are you shy? Promiscuous? Cold and angry? Polite but distant? Demanding? Where did that begin?

WINDOW

The old Dickens favorite *A Christmas Carol* is really all about this issue. Scrooge has become a cold and hard miser because of how he handled the Arrows of his youth. The Ghost of Christmas Past takes him back to his youth so that he might see what has happened and grieve the sorrow. It's such a powerful story. I think of Longfellow's line, "Often times we call a man cold when he is only sad."[16]

How about the way you relate to yourself? How do you treat yourself? Are you always down on yourself? Do you demand perfection? (Perhaps you've come to see yourself as the victim and make excuses for everything you do.)

And what about the way you relate to God? Do you find it hard to trust him with the things you most deeply care about? Do you secretly fear him?

A WAY TOWARD HEALING

Your Arrows, their messages, and the way you handled them do not have to be the end of the story. (After all, we're only in chapter 3—that ought to give you some hope!) You do not have to be ruled by it all. Read the following passage from Isaiah 61:1–3 slowly, carefully. Speaking of Jesus, the prophet wrote:

The Spirit of the Sovereign Lord is on me,
because the Lord has anointed me
to proclaim good news to the poor.
He has sent me to bind up the brokenhearted,
to proclaim freedom for the captives
and release from darkness for the prisoners,
to proclaim the year of the Lord's favor
and the day of vengeance of our God,
to comfort all who mourn,
and provide for those who grieve in Zion—
to bestow on them a crown of beauty
instead of ashes,
the oil of joy
instead of mourning,
and a garment of praise
instead of a spirit of despair.

This is the passage that Jesus quoted when he stepped onto the stage in Luke 4. This, he said, is why he had come. Let's take him at his word. Let's begin the path toward healing.

RENOUNCE THE VOW

The only thing more tragic than the tragedy that happens to us is the way we handle it—the choices we make, the person we become, the life we live (or don't live). Jesus said, "Whosoever shall seek to save his life shall lose it" (Luke 17:33 KJV). The things we do to protect and preserve our hearts usually end up hurting us more. To choose to shut your heart to love—so that you won't be hurt—is to deny the very thing you are made for. To demand perfection of yourself so that no one will ever criticize you again is to lay an intolerable burden on your back.

We must renounce our vows.

Childhood vows are very dangerous things. They trap our hearts, pin them down. They act almost like covenants between us and the evil one. You see, he is the father of lies. His major work is to destroy us by getting us to agree with his lies. The wound is the way he gets the agreement. The pain makes the message of the Arrow seem so true, so deep inside, we believe the lie and make the vow. It is very important to break childhood vows so that the evil one can no longer have a stronghold in our hearts.

$$=== \text{IF YOU ARE FEELING} \dots ===$$

"The evil one? You mean Satan? What's he got to do with all this?" We will have much more to say about his role in the story later. For now, listen to Ephesians 4:26–27: "'In your anger do not sin': Do not let the sun go down while you are still angry, and do not give the devil a foothold." Unresolved emotional wounds create spiritual strongholds in our hearts. Quite often for healing to really be complete, we must renounce the place we've given the lie and the liar. That's why we renounce the vow.

This is something between you and God. It doesn't have to be dramatic. In prayer, acknowledge the vow you once made. Renounce it once and for all. Ask Jesus to defend your heart.

GRIEVE THE WOUND

Remember the story Brent told about going back as a young man to the farm, the bridge, and the creek that meant so much to him as a boy? It hurt so much to see it all gone, so he used cold anger to kill the last of the longing in his heart. Why do we do such things to ourselves? "I know now I placed that last Arrow in my heart that day and shoved it cleanly through. I did it to kill the tears of mourning inside." Brent wrote that if he had allowed the loss to flow "in the waters of my own tears," then he wouldn't have lost his heart and the Romance with it.

It is so important for us to grieve our losses. It is the only honest thing to do. For in grieving we admit the truth: We lost something very dear, and it hurt us very much. Tears are healing. They help to open and cleanse the wound. Augustine wrote in his *Confessions*, "The tears . . . streamed down, and I let them flow as freely as they would, making of them a pillow for my heart. On them it rested."

It might be helpful in your grieving to make for yourself an Inventory of Loss. As you look back over your Arrows and their messages and the way they shaped your life, think about what you have lost. What was lost when the Arrow struck? What has been lost since then?

People you no longer have
Relationships that ended
Dreams unfulfilled
So much life you have not lived

As you linger over the loss and recall the pain of the Arrows, let your grief happen. Use your journal to record it.

Now I want you to do something very simple. Ask the Lord to heal your broken heart. Invite him into that place in your heart, to cleanse, to heal, and to mend. Pray through Isaiah 61:1–3. Ask him to do those very things for you, for this place in your heart. He will. It's what he said he came to do: "Blessed are those who mourn, for they *will* be comforted" (Matthew 5:4, emphasis added).

WINDOW

John Michael Talbot has a beautiful song entitled "Healer of My Soul." It goes like this:

Healer of my soul
Heal me at morning
Heal me at noon
Heal me at even
Healer of my soul.

I am tired
Afraid and stumbling
Heal my soul

I've often played it as a prayer when I needed God to heal my soul.

REJECT THE MESSAGE

Finally, we must reject the lie that has so long defined us. Have you ever stopped to ask yourself whether the messages of those Arrows are *true*? Because of the wound, because the message was delivered by an Arrow, it sinks in deep and feels authoritative. But the fact is, nearly every message of every Arrow is untrue. You are loved. You are not alone. God does care.

This is where the truth really does set us free. Jesus said that in John 8:32. But as Jesus also said, we must hold to the truth, *cling* to it in order for it to set us free (see verse 31). Go back over every one of your messages that you wrote. Ask the Holy Spirit to reveal to you what's really true. Search the Scriptures for the answer to those lies. You don't have to passively accept them anymore.

For example, here are some common lies . . . and the truths to counter them:

I am on my own: *"Never will I leave you; never will I forsake you"* (Hebrews 13:5).

I am unlovely and unloved: *"I have loved you with an everlasting love"* (Jeremiah 31:3).

God doesn't care about me: *"God demonstrates his own love for us in this . . . Christ died for us"* (Romans 5:8).

TO CLARIFY

I don't want to create a wrong impression through these exercises. Dealing with your Arrows is rarely something that can be done in one night or one chapter. This is a beginning. You may need help to sort through all this. Turning to a counselor for help is not a sign of weakness; in fact, it takes great courage. But it can be life-changing.

Either way, this process will come and go in your journey of the heart. New Arrows will strike; old ones long forgotten will resurface. What I offer here is the way toward healing.

WINDOWS

Film
Shadowlands (Savoy Pictures, 1993).

A River Runs Through It (Columbia Pictures, 1993).

Music
Again, when it comes to personal recollections, there is no substitute for the music we loved when we were young—"the soundtrack of our lives." As with the last chapter, you might find listening to some of your old favorites helpful in this part of the journey.

"Adagio for Strings" by Samuel Barber. This may be one of the most haunting, sad, and beautiful pieces of music in the world. Many, many recordings are available. It was also used for the soundtrack of *Platoon*, the tragic Vietnam War movie.

Shadowlands motion picture soundtrack (Angel Records, 1994). Especially tracks 15, 17, and 21.

"On My Own," from the musical *Les Misérables*. I prefer the London cast recording (Polydor Records, 1988).

"Healer of My Soul" by John Michael Talbot, from *The God of Life* (Troubadour for the Lord, 1984). Also available on *John Michael Talbot Collection* (EMI/Capitol, 1995) and *Brother to Brother* (Sony/Word, 1996).

Photo Albums
Take a personal journey to your past by spending an evening looking at photos from your youth. Keep your journal nearby. I don't want to pour it on, but you might try listening to "Adagio for Strings" or *Shadowlands* as background music.

Places
You may live within driving distance of the places that were significant to you as a child. You may want to visit them again, as Brent went back to the farm, or as others visit gravesides. (Take your journal with you.)

Books

The Healing Path by Dan Allender (Colorado Springs, CO: WaterBrook, 1999). The subtitle should clue you in: *How the Hurts in Your Past Can Lead You to a More Abundant Life.*

The Heart's Desire by James Houston (Oxford, UK: Lion Books, 1992). Especially chapters 6 and 7.

Lament for a Son by Nicholas Wolterstorf (Grand Rapids, MI: William B. Eerdmans, 1987). Written after the death of his twenty-five-year-old son in a mountaineering accident, this is the best book I've read in helping me with my own grief.

4

A STORY BIG ENOUGH TO LIVE IN

Romance is the deepest thing in life; romance is deeper even than reality.

G. K. CHESTERTON[17]

YOUR INITIAL REACTION

In two or three minutes, jot down the things that struck you when you read this chapter. What were your initial thoughts, emotions, impressions?

I felt . . .

I realized . . .

I wanted . . .

PRAYER OF BEGINNING

*Show me your ways, L*ORD*,*
   teach me your paths.
Guide me in your truth and teach me,
   for you are God my Savior (Psalm 25:4-5).

Dear Jesus, show me the ways that I have chosen to live. Reveal to me how I have written a smaller story for myself—a safer one. Enable me to see the way in which I try to control the Arrows and arrange for a little bit of Romance. And speak to me about the story you are telling, the story I am truly made for. Open my eyes, Lord. In your name I pray. Amen.

TO CLARIFY

Here are the central truths of this chapter:

- We must find a way to make sense of, to reconcile, the Arrows and the Romance.
- Life makes sense only as a story, but most of the stories we choose are too "small" for our hearts.
- Modern Christianity doesn't seem at all like the great story we need; it just seems like tips and techniques.
- But Christianity is actually like a great fairy tale—only it's true.

TRYING TO FIGURE OUT LIFE

Chapter 4 is about how we make sense of the mixed messages of our lives. "Who gets the last word—the Romance or the Arrows?" Is life a wonderful story of love and adventure? Or was Macbeth right? Is it "a tale told by an idiot, full of sound and fury, signifying nothing"?[18] Which seems most true to you? In the past year, which answer have you mostly agreed with?

No one can live with Macbeth's answer (though many of us wind up there, down in our heart of hearts). It's not just that we want to know how to deal with the Arrows and hang on to the Romance—but also we need to. For the sake of our hearts, we *must* resolve our dilemmas. The problem, however, is that "most of us live our lives like a movie we've arrived at twenty minutes late. . . . We sense that something really important, perhaps even glorious, is taking place, and yet it all seems so *random*. Beauty catches us by surprise and makes us wish for more, but then the Arrows come and we are pierced."

Does your life seem random to you? Can you predict if a day is going to be good or bad? Does life ever feel like "the riddle of the earth," as Chesterton put it?[19]

Dallas Willard wrote in *The Divine Conspiracy*, "Meaning is not a luxury for us. It is a kind of spiritual oxygen . . . that enables our souls to live."[20] Are you comfortable living life as a riddle, or do you struggle to make sense of things? Is your heart satisfied with the answers you've come up with?

LISTEN TO YOUR HEART

A. W. Tozer said that our real beliefs lie buried *beneath* our doctrines and creeds.[21] What does your *heart* believe about life's story?

OUR INTERPRETERS

When we are young, we do not have the ability to make sense of the way life unfolds. This is especially true when tragedy strikes. We turn to those whom we trust, typically our parents or grandparents or other authority figures, to help us interpret our experiences. Think of the people who most influenced you as a child. How did they "make sense" of life? Specifically, what did they teach you about the Arrows, the Romance, and what to do with your own heart?

IF YOU ARE FEELING . . .

But I don't remember much of anything my parents taught me about life. Yes, it is a rare parent indeed who teaches his child about the crucial issues in life with clarity and kindness. Most of what we learn, we learn by *example.* Many of us heard, "Listen to what I say, not what I do." But we do quite the opposite. Think about the way your parents *lived,* and you will discover what they taught you.

For example, I noticed recently that I have a tendency, when I'm feeling low, to buy something. I suddenly realized that is exactly how my mom handled her troubles. Although she never told me to deal with pain that way, it's exactly what I learned from her.

Let me help you be more specific. Using your mother, your father, and another key person in your life (a grandparent, a teacher, or perhaps an older sibling you looked up to), how did they handle their own Arrows? Did they talk about them? Were tears openly shared in your home? Or were things swept under the rug? Perhaps they were overcome by their sorrows. What did that teach you? And what did they tell you to do with your Arrows?

Mom

Dad

Another key person

Carl Jung said that there is no stronger psychological influence on a child than "the unlived life of the parent."[22] How did each of your parents handle the longings we all have for the Romance? Was laughter common in your home? Was adventure encouraged? Did they live their dreams? Abandon them? Or were things focused on the practical, on surviving? And what did they tell you to do with your search for the Romance?

Mom

Dad

Another key person

Whose approach to life do you feel you adopted? Or was no one there at all to help you interpret your experience? As I said in the book, "I was left entirely on my own to form my understanding of the story of life and my role in it." If that was true for you as well, how has that shaped you?

OUR NEED FOR A STORY

The importance of the idea of story will grow as we move through the book. "Story," as I said, "is the language of the heart." Is that a new thought to you? Does it strike you as an odd thought or a true thought?

Let's explore just how significant story is to us. Imagine that it's Friday night, after a long, hard week. You have a free evening before you. Would you rather watch a great movie or review principles on time management?

Picture yourself at home on a snowy Sunday afternoon. You've built a fire in the fireplace. The house is quiet, and you have several hours of private time ahead. Would you like to curl up with your tax return?

An old and dear friend has come to town and asked you to dinner. It has been years since you've been together, and there is so much catching up to do. There's a new love; they've been on a European vacation; and they said something in their letter about "knowing God more deeply." Would you rather that they simply tell you the facts about their lives, so you can hurry up and be finished with it? Or do you look forward to hearing the stories?

Now flip through your Bible for a moment. How much of God's Word to us is written like a tax return form or auto repair manual, and how much of it is written as story?

═══ TO CLARIFY ═══

People wonder why the novel is the most popular form of literature; people wonder why it is read more than books of science or books [on spirituality]. The reason is very simple; it is merely that the novel is more true than they are. Our existence may cease to be a song; it may cease even to be a beautiful lament . . . But our existence is still a story.

G. K. CHESTERTON, "ON CERTIN MODERN WRITERS
AND THE INSTITUTION OF THE FAMILY"

You are your stories. You are the product of all the stories you have heard and lived. . . . They shape how you see yourself, the world, and your place in it.

DANIEL TAYLOR, *THE HEALING POWER OF STORIES*[23]

Stories are equipment for living.

ROBERT MCKEE, *STORY*[24]

If your life *could* become a great story—if you could live in one of your favorite movies—which would you choose? Why?

How close to your present life does that movie feel? Do you think you'll ever get there? Is there another movie your life *does* feel like?

Think back to the stories you loved as a child. How relevant do they seem to your life now?

TO CLARIFY

None of the "big questions" will ever be news. . . . The product of the news business is *change*, not wisdom. You need to go elsewhere for wisdom. Wisdom has to do with seeing things in their largest context, whereas news is structured in a way that destroys the larger context. . . . If readers were aware of the bigger story it would diminish today's contribution to that story. So news-industry profits absolutely depend on dumbing us down by deconstructing our world by dailiness.

C. JOHN SOMMERVILLE, *HOW THE NEWS MAKES US DUMB*[25]

Even the church has lost the story. "We have lived for so long with a 'propositional' approach to Christianity we have nearly lost its true meaning." How does your church present Christianity? As a great drama, a love story set in the midst of a life-and-death struggle? Or is the focus more on teaching principles?

WINDOW

In their song "Hero," David Crosby and Phil Collins capture the longing I believe all people feel for a story that makes sense. The first stanza goes like this:

> It was one of those great stories
> That you can't put down at night
> The hero knew what he had to do
> And he wasn't afraid to fight
> The villain goes to jail
> While the hero goes free
> I wish it were that simple for me.

CREATING OUR OWN STORY

"So, what are we left to do? Create our own story line to bring some meaning to our experiences. Our heart is made to live in a larger story; having lost that we do the best we can by developing smaller dramas." Let's explore that idea a bit. We know that plot, character, and setting are the three basic elements of any story. Take, for example, the simple nursery rhyme about Jack and Jill: Jack and Jill (the characters) went up a hill (the setting) to fetch a pail of water (the plot).

Using these three elements, think about your life for a few moments. Put some words to how you see yourself and your situation.

Character
What role are you playing? How do you see your part? Are you a victim of cruel circumstances? A key player? A survivor?

Imagine that Hollywood is going to make a movie of your life. Which actor do you hope the director would cast to play you? On the other hand, which actor do you fear the director would choose to play you? (I *want* to be seen as a Daniel Craig 007 action hero. I *fear* I'll be revealed to be like the goofy character Ernest—a boy trying to play a man.)

Plot

What is life about? What's really happening here? Is life a tragedy? A game? A marathon? A shopping spree? How do you basically see it?

Think back to the earlier question I asked about a movie you would love to live in and the movie you see as closer to your life. What's the plot of the second story, the one you see as yours?

Often, our interpreters teach us the meaning of life through a saying they frequently quote or a motto they would live by. "When life hands you lemons, make lemonade" would be one example. "God helps those who help themselves" would be another. Can you remember such a slogan or motto that was important to your parents or other key people in your life? Can you recall a time when they passed it on to you? That's probably how you see the plot.

We must not forget that culture is a powerful tutor. From a very young age, most of us have been exposed to the mottos of our culture through music, television, movies, and so on. Quite often, if there is not a strong interpreter in the home, a young person will learn his outlook on life from popular culture. (This is especially true in the teenage years.) Every generation comes up with its own mottos. Is there a bumper sticker that sums up your outlook on life? (Do you have one on your car?)

Setting

Shakespeare wrote, "All the world's a stage, and all the men and women merely players."[26] What kind of world do you feel you live in? What is the stage itself like? Is it a fearful place? A big playground? A jungle?

More specifically, does the world you live in account for both the natural and the supernatural? How involved is God on a day-to-day basis? Do you expect to encounter him or an angel at any moment?

OUR STORY IS NOT LARGE ENOUGH

Depending on our temperament and how life has unfolded for us, I believe we choose either a story that focuses on controlling the Arrows or one that tries to hang on to the Romance. Looking at your story, can you see which applies to you?

"Through baseball and politics and music and sex and even church, we are searching desperately for a larger story in which to live and find our role. All of these smaller stories offer a taste of meaning, adventure, or connectedness. But none of them offer the real thing; they aren't large enough." The reason is this: As human beings, we need a past that was planned for us and a future that waits for us. Does your story build on a wonderful past? Does it anticipate an even more wonderful future?

Without a larger story, we end up trapped in the present, looking for a sense of being alive now, for now is all we have. Be honest. How much of each week is pretty much focused on the "here and now"?

WINDOW

In the movie *Groundhog Day,* Bill Murray plays a conceited weatherman covering the famous groundhog ceremony from a small town in Pennsylvania. He finds himself condemned to live the day over and over again, caught in a sort of time warp. Resigned to his fate, he tries every small story he can think of, living out every role he ever wanted. When they all fail him, he discovers the real meaning of life. It's the book of Ecclesiastes in a modern film.

THE SACRED ROMANCE

Only one kind of story offers the explanation we've been seeking: the fairy tale. As I said in this chapter, "Children aren't a bad place to look when we're trying to get beyond the cynicism of adulthood and so it shouldn't surprise us that most children have found a way of reconciling the messages. Before skepticism takes over (what we mistakenly call maturity) children intuit the true story as fairy tale."

Now here is an interesting question: When was the last time you enjoyed fairy tales? Do they seem immature to you? What does that say about how you view maturity?

TO CLARIFY

"As far as I know," wrote Frederick Buechner in *Telling the Truth: The Gospel as Tragedy, Comedy, and Fairy Tale,* "there has never been an age that has not produced fairy tales." There is something deeply true about a fairy tale. It is a timeless form of storytelling because it captures a timeless story. Fairy tales employ universal symbolism that captures both our deepest fears and our highest hopes. They help us understand the meaning of life in a way nothing else does.

Buechner added: "Maybe the first thing to say is that it is a world full of darkness and danger and ambiguity . . . There are fierce dragons who guard the treasure and wicked fairies who show up at royal christenings. To take the wrong turning of the path is to risk being lost in the forest forever, and an awful price has to be paid for choosing the wrong casket or the wrong door. It is a world of dark and dangerous quest where the suitors compete for the hand of the king's daughter with death to the losers, or the young prince searches for the princess who has slept for a hundred years, or the scarecrow, the tin man, and the lion travel many a mile in search of the wizard who will make them whole, and all of them encounter on their way great perils that are all the more perilous because they are seldom seen for what they are.

"Good and evil meet and do battle in the fairy-tale world much as they meet and do battle in our world, but in fairy tales the good live happily ever after. That is the major difference."[27]

Think of your favorite fairy tales. Is there danger? Is evil given a role? Is there a hero or heroine? Does good triumph in the end? Can you see there the themes of the gospel?

WINDOW

Watch Disney's movie *Sleeping Beauty*. Notice the striking parallels to the gospel. The villain looks like a beautiful queen, but she turns into a dragon. Satan, we are told, comes as an angel of light but is revealed as a dragon in Revelation 12. The hero is a prince who does battle for his bride. Has not Christ—the Prince of Peace—come to battle for us, the bride of Christ? And the kingdom is under a spell until it is broken by love.

The Sacred Romance is our way of expressing the great fairy tale that God is telling. It helps us understand where the Arrows have come from by teaching us about the evil villain and his ways. It also helps us stay alive to the Romance, knowing that the Haunting we experience is God wooing our hearts to a love affair. Have you ever thought of Christianity as a great and true fairy tale? What difference would it make to your faith and your life if you did?

LISTEN TO YOUR HEART

One young woman admitted to me that she sees her life only as a tragic story. When she heard the message of the Sacred Romance, she said, "Oh, if only it were true. I ache to believe it's true."

WINDOWS

Film

Groundhog Day (Columbia/TriStar, 1997).

Sleeping Beauty (Walt Disney, 1959).

Music

Dances with Wolves motion picture soundtrack (CBS Records, 1990). Especially tracks 3, 4, 10, and 17.

"Hero" by David Crosby and Phil Collins, from *Thousand Roads* (Atlantic Records, 1993).

Books

The Healing Power of Stories by Daniel Taylor (New York: Doubleday, 1996). In chapter 1, Taylor makes this astounding point: "If your present life story is broken or diseased, it can be made well. Or, if necessary, it can be replaced by a story that has a plot worth living."

Orthodoxy by G. K. Chesterton (many editions available). Especially chapter 4, "The Ethics of Elfland." It is there that Chesterton describes his own coming to see Christianity as a fairy tale.

5

THE WILDNESS OF GOD

[We live our lives before the] wild, dangerous, unfettered, and free . . .
character of [the living God].

WALTER BRUEGGEMANN[28]

YOUR INITIAL REACTION

In two or three minutes, jot down the things that struck you when you read this chapter. What were your initial thoughts, emotions, impressions?

I felt . . .

I realized . . .

I wanted . . .

PRAYER OF BEGINNING

Why, Lord, do you stand far off?
Why do you hide yourself in times of trouble? (Psalm 10:1).

Dear Jesus, I have to admit that often I do not understand your ways. I believe you are good, or at least, I want to believe you are good. But I struggle with what you allow to go on down here. What sort of story are you writing, Lord? What is my part in it? Help me to be honest with you, and lift my eyes to see beyond the story I have written. In your name I pray. Amen.

TO CLARIFY

Here are the central truths of this chapter:

- Deep in our hearts, we all carry a hidden question: "Do you care about me, God?"
- Like Job, we try to control the wildness of God through careful living, but God is not "safe."
- His wildness redeems us from our smaller "self-redemptive" stories.
- And we have been given a far larger part in a much bigger drama than we ever imagined.

THE QUESTION IN OUR HEART

I ended the last chapter by inviting you to explore "the drama that God has been weaving since before the beginning of time, which he has also placed in our heart. Who are the main players in this larger story? What is the plot? How do we fit in? As we rediscover the oldest story in the world, one that is forever young, we journey into the heart of God and toward the recovery of our own hearts. For perhaps God would be reason enough to stay open to the Romance if we knew he would keep us safe. And therein we experience a great fear and confusion."

The fear and confusion are simply this: If God is writing a Romance for us, if we are made to live in a fairy tale, then why did he allow all those Arrows we talked about in chapter 3? What Arrows will he permit in the future? As Brent said, somewhere deep down inside we wonder, *"'God, why did you allow this to happen to me? Why did you make me like this? What will you allow to happen next?'* In the secret places of our heart, we believe God is the One who did not protect us from these things or even the One who perpetrated them upon us. Our questions about him make us begin to live with a deep apprehension that clings anxiously to the depths of our hearts . . . *'Do you really care for me, God?'"*

Have you ever felt that "deep apprehension"? As you try to open your heart to the Romance, do you sense it even now?

LISTEN TO YOUR HEART

If you really care for me, God, then why did you . . . ? We suppress this question as long as we can. All of us. But listen to your heart. What happens inside when you think of completely trusting him? The apprehension is there.

Brent remembered this apprehension and this question forming thanks to playground bullies from his days at Crockett Elementary. He said, "No one came"; he wasn't rescued from the situation. What were the events that began to surface this question for you? Have recent events brought the question back?

Perhaps life has gone well for you. I'm grateful. Truly grateful. But what do you do with the way other people's lives have turned out? What do you do with the Holocaust, for example? Or the unspeakable suffering of children? As Brent wrote, the things that have happened to us or to our loved ones "often suggest that the real script of the play we're all living in is 'God is indifferent' rather than 'God is love.'" Have you ever felt that way? Are you comfortable admitting it?

IF YOU ARE FEELING . . .

It's just not okay to voice thoughts like these. Many people feel this way. I certainly have. But take another look through the Psalms. They are *filled* with this question. Again and again and again the psalmists take their doubts to God:

> How long, LORD? Will you forget me forever?
> How long will you hide your face from me? (Psalm 13:1).

> My God, my God, why have you forsaken me?
> Why are you so far from saving me,
> so far from my cries of anguish? (Psalm 22:1).

> Why do you hide your face
> and forget our misery and oppression? (Psalm 44:24).

Those were godly men who openly voiced their doubts to God. In fact, Psalm 22 is the one Jesus quoted from the cross. Their example *invites* us to voice our questions. It's the only way we'll ever deal with them,

"But I don't have questions like these about God." Hmmm. It may be true that you have never allowed the questions to *surface*, but to say you have no doubts about God places you above some pretty extraordinary men of the Bible, including King David, who was a man "after [God's] own heart" (1 Samuel 13:14), and Job, who was "blameless and upright . . . the greatest man among all the people of the East" (Job 1:1, 3).

In your heart of hearts, do you see God as a great Romancer inviting us to a life of wonder and love? What is your picture of God? What kind of story *is* he writing for you?

WINDOW

In the movie *The Truman Show*, we are given a story of a man whose life is manipulated by a powerful but uncaring "god." Truman is actually the only character in a television show who doesn't know his life is a television show. Every moment of every day has been carefully arranged for the pleasure of the viewing audience. The director of the show is named Christof (notice the inference to Christ). He has Truman trapped in a story that really doesn't have his best interests in mind. And when Truman tries to break out of his artificial world, Christof tries to thwart him and even take his life.

It's a picture that many people have of God—up there somewhere, pulling all the strings, but not really caring about us, whose story he controls.

WHEN *GOOD* DOES NOT EQUATE SAFE

What do you make of the behind-the-scenes story of Job, where God and Satan essentially battle it out through the life of this unsuspecting man? Do you like it?

We know God is good. At least, that's what the Bible tells us on nearly every page. And all of us "would like to picture goodness as being synonymous with safety." Don't you want to believe that God is safe? Don't you want to believe that he will grant you immunity from life's Arrows and hardships?

—— LISTEN TO ——
YOUR HEART

Haven't you always sensed that God is out of your control? Have you felt comfortable admitting it?

Why are we so apprehensive about conceding that God is "wild"? Why do we so prefer a God to whom we can relate through formulas?

TO CLARIFY

You may have a hard time with the word *wild*. I do. It raises all kinds of questions I'd rather not deal with. But I want to make sure you aren't struggling with God's wildness because you misunderstand what we mean and are equating that word with others bearing a *different* meaning.

Synonyms for *wild* that we *don't* mean:

> *Irresponsible*
>
> *Capricious*
>
> *Unfeeling*
>
> *Unprincipled*
>
> *Chaotic*

Synonyms for *wild* that we *do* mean:

> *Untamed*
>
> *Out of our control*
>
> *Not bound by formulas*
>
> *Unpredictable*
>
> *Inherently risky*

WINDOW

If you have not read *The Lion, the Witch and the Wardrobe* by C. S. Lewis, you must. It's the first book in his series called the Chronicles of Narnia. (Recent editions of the series put *The Lion* second, after *The Magician's Nephew*. But that is not the way Lewis wanted it. Read *The Lion* first.) In his character Aslan, the great lion, Lewis gives us a picture of Christ that is somehow more rich and true than most Sunday school portraits.

REACHING OUT FOR CONTROL

Do you see now why Job was so careful in his religion? What motivated him to be so diligent in his "regular custom" of religious observance (see Job 1:5; 3:25)?

The "household god" approach that Brent refers to has been very common throughout human history. The basic plan is A + B = C. Do this and that and then your god *has* to come through for you. What was the formula of Job's friend Eliphaz for relating to God?

Do you think we're free of that approach today? Has anyone ever said to you something like what Eliphaz said to Job?

What about your spiritual life? Is there anything you do that might be attempting the same thing—to control the wildness of God? Might a custom of regular devotions or church attendance or moral living be motivated by the same sort of fear that was in Job's heart—that if you don't, something bad will happen?

What do you fear will "come upon" you?

A STRANGE *REDEMPTION*

Brent asks one of life's most crucial questions in this chapter: "What are we to make of God's wildness in allowing these things to happen?" (By "these things," he means all the risk and wildness and tragedies of life.) What *have* you made of it? Before reading this chapter, how would you have answered the question, "Why does God act so wild?"

=== **TO CLARIFY** ===

If God is all-loving and all-powerful, he could stop the tragedies of my life. But he doesn't. So, the argument goes, either he doesn't really care, or he doesn't have the power to do anything about it. In *When Bad Things Happen to Good People,* Rabbi Harold S. Kushner basically concludes that God cares, but he's not powerful enough to help.[29] Many Christians live with a similar belief. But that is not the God of the Bible. He is all-powerful. He asks the Israelites, "Do I lack the strength to rescue you?" (Isaiah 50:2).

Those who hang on to God's sovereignty often fall into the belief that he doesn't really care. *Oh, he loves others, but not me.* It's impossible to hold that conviction after the cross, however. Nobody has ever loved you enough to die for you.

Actually, I think we've quite misunderstood the power of love. We think it's merely being "nice." *If God loved me, he'd leave me to be happy.* Not at all. He loves you too much to leave you the way you are. George MacDonald said, "Love loves unto purity. Love has ever in view the absolute loveliness of that which it beholds. . . . All that comes between and is not of love's kind, must be destroyed. And our God is a consuming fire."[30] I think of the powerful story told by Sheldon Vanauken in *A Severe Mercy*. He lost his beloved wife to a serious liver disease. Yet he saw in it the redemption of God. For their love was so intense that while they were together, no one could get in—not even God himself.

After admitting his outrage and anxiety over how God treated Job, Brent confessed that what he really wanted to do was "ask for a much smaller part in the play than Job had; or possibly even a role in a more off-Broadway production that I could help direct. You know, something like *God Helps Brent Pursue Money, Wealth, and Fame While Living a Quiet Life*." Can you relate? Write a title to the story you wish God would let you direct for your life.

If we're honest with ourselves, we have to admit that we "are convinced at some level in our heart that our main difficulty is the capriciousness of life. . . . The way we want to live feels so right—so much like life—the only problem seems to be the way others treat us and God's indifference to our pleas for help." Isn't that true? If God could change right now three things about your life, what would you ask for? List them. Aren't they a change in circumstances or in others around you? (Remember, be honest with all these questions. Don't try to make them sound spiritual, mature, or "right.")

Think back to the exercises in chapter 4, the story you've created and the role you are playing. How necessary is it that God "show up" for things to work out?

Certainly we would all love to have God come through for us. But is it *essential* to your plan, or is God more of a backup if you can't get your story to work?

Notice something else about your smaller story. Who is the central character? Though we as Christians might want to *say* that God is the central figure, is he really the central figure in your story? For example, after your quiet time or your morning prayer, how much of your day do you spend watching for what God is up to and how much just trying to get on top of things?

Referring to the movie *Forrest Gump*, Brent describes Lieutenant Dan's smaller story as "self-redemptive" because Dan sees it as his only way to "recognition, honor, self-respect—indeed, salvation." Why does God take his smaller story away?

WINDOW

The scenes of Lieutenant Dan's redemption are found in the movie *Forrest Gump*. You might want to watch the movie, especially focusing on this character's encounter with God. By the close of the film, what happens in Lieutenant Dan's heart, thanks to the wildness of God?

When God takes away Lieutenant Dan's story, the man is filled with shame, anger, and despair. Think back to a recent event that made you feel shame, anger, or despair. Why? What did you lose? What aspect of your story was taken away?

—— **LISTEN TO** ——
YOUR HEART

What aspect of your story do
you fear will be taken away next
by this wild God? What does
that say about where you think
your life is found?

The wildness of God has a purpose. It is a strange *redemption*. "The story of Lieutenant Dan is a poignant and revealing portrayal of God's fierce intentions to use both crippling and blessing to redeem us from our self-redemptive and purgatorial stories." Think about God's refusal to cooperate with your smaller story. What is currently not working about your story? What might he be trying to save you from?

═══ **IF YOU ARE FEELING . . .** ═══

I don't really see what God is up to. It just seems that I'm experiencing trials. Yes, I often feel like that too. But if you'll look a bit more carefully, you'll see that the trials in your life have a *pattern* to them. And when you look at your smaller story, the way in which you try to arrange your life, you'll make the connection. May I suggest a simple prayer?

Dear God, I know you are up to something in my life. But all it feels like right now is just hardship and difficulty. Open my eyes. Show me what you are after. Show me the way you are trying to redeem me. Amen.

A PART TOO LARGE

One thing is for sure: God loves *drama*. Brent notes, "God calls us to battles where the deck appears to be stacked in favor of those who are his enemies and ours, just to increase the drama of the play." Look back over the major stories in the Bible. Do you see how God loves last-minute deliverances? The Israelites are pinned against the Red Sea, with Pharaoh and his army charging down on them—then God shows up. Abraham raises the knife to kill Isaac—then God shows up. Shadrach, Meshach, and Abednego are thrown into the fiery furnace—then God shows up. Jesus is crucified, and a stone seals the tomb . . . you get the idea. How does it make you feel to know that the God who wrote those stories is writing yours?

━━━ WINDOW ━━━

In his song "Show the Way," David Wilcox offers an explanation for life that brings together both the Romance and the Arrows and our part in it. He sees it all as a great drama, written by Love:

> Look, if someone wrote a play just to glorify
> What's stronger than hate, would they not arrange the stage
> To look as if the hero came too late he's almost in defeat
> It's looking like the Evil side will win, so on the Edge
> Of every seat, from the moment that the whole thing begins
> It is . . .
>
> Love who makes the mortar
> And it's love who stacked these stones
> And it's love who made the stage here
> Although it looks like we're alone
> In this scene set in shadows

Like the night is here to stay
There is evil cast around us
But it's love who wrote the play
For in this darkness love can show the way.

Did Job have any idea how large a part he was playing? For that matter, did the four children in *The Lion, the Witch and the Wardrobe* have any idea that they were key players in that story? Do you sense *you* are playing a crucial role, "center stage in a drama of cosmic proportions"?

What if you are? What if you have been cast in a role as significant as the characters in Narnia or in the Bible, people like Job and Jeremiah and Paul? How would it affect the way you see your life?

What is preventing you from accepting that as fact—from allowing it to be true that you are key to a far larger, far wilder, and yet far more wonderful story than the one you've tried to write?

═══ TO CLARIFY ═══

In his book *Heretics*, G. K. Chesterton makes a crucial observation about stories of romance and heroism: "But in order that life should be a story or romance to us, it is necessary that a great part of it, at any rate, should be settled for us without our permission. If we wish life to be a system, this may be a nuisance; but if we wish it to be a drama, it is an essential."

Chesterton goes on to admit that we may not like what is being written:

> But we should like it still less if the author came before the curtain every hour or so, and forced on us the whole trouble of inventing the next act. A man has control over many things in his life; he has control over enough things to be the hero of a novel. But if he had control over everything, there would be so much hero that there would be no novel . . .
>
> The thing which keeps life romantic and full of fiery possibilities is the existence of these great plain limitations which force all of us to meet the things we do not like or do not expect.[31]

WINDOWS

Film

Forrest Gump (Paramount Pictures, 1995).

The Truman Show (Paramount Pictures, 1998).

Music

The Last of the Mohicans motion picture soundtrack (Morgan Creek Music, 1992). Especially tracks 1, 2, and 16.

"Show the Way" by David Wilcox, from *Big Horizon* (A&M Records, 1994).

Books

The God Who Risks by John Sanders (InterVarsity Press, 1998). A very provocative book, as the title suggests.

The Lion, the Witch and the Wardrobe by C. S. Lewis (New York: HarperCollins, 2008).

A Severe Mercy by Sheldon Vanauken (San Francisco: HarperSanFrancisco, 1992).

6

GOD THE AGELESS ROMANCER

So long as we imagine it is we who have to look for God, we must often lose heart. But it is the other way about—He is looking for us.

SIMON TUGWELL[32]

YOUR INITIAL REACTION

In two or three minutes, jot down the things that struck you when you read this chapter. What were your initial thoughts, emotions, impressions?

I felt . . .

I realized . . .

I wanted . . .

PRAYER OF BEGINNING

You have searched me, Lᴏʀᴅ,
and you know me.
You know when I sit and when I rise;
you perceive my thoughts from afar. . . .
Where can I go from your Spirit?
Where can I flee from your presence?
If I go up to the heavens, you are there;
if I make my bed in the depths, you are there.
If I rise on the wings of the dawn,
if I settle on the far side of the sea,
even there your hand will guide me,
your right hand will hold me fast (Psalm 139:1-2, 7-10).

Dear Jesus, it seems too good to be true. Are you really pursuing me? Have you really been pursuing me all these years? Help me to believe it. Speak these truths to my heart in a deep and personal way. Let the years of fear and doubt melt away in the presence of your passionate love for me. In your name I pray. Amen.

TO CLARIFY

Here are the central truths of this chapter:

- The only way we can trust such a wild Lover is to know that his heart is good.
- We see God's heart only when we look at the larger story with God as its hero.
- What we discover when we do is a jealous Lover who has been pursuing us from before time began.
- And life is revealed to be the great Romance we have longed for it to be.

WHAT KIND OF HEART DOES GOD HAVE?

In this chapter, we search for the heart of God. We must. Faced with the uncertainty of life, many of us have turned to God in hope that he will make the Arrows go away and arrange for just a little more blessing in our lives. After all, he's God. He's the Author of the play. If he wanted to, he could rescue us and carry us to safety. But we find in God Someone far more wild than we had hoped for, Someone far beyond our control. All our questions ultimately come down to one: *How can I trust a Lover who is so wild?*

WINDOW

The wildness of God—and the position his wildness leaves us in—is captured in the scene I describe from the movie *The Last of the Mohicans*, where Nathaniel leaps from the waterfall, leaving Cora behind to be seized by the enemy. It's a very powerful scene, and it raises our core question about the wildness of God. You might want to watch the scene yourself, putting yourself in Cora's shoes. What is she feeling? How is she able to carry on?

"Indeed," I ask, "how do we not only trust him, but love him in return?" Let me pose a rather frank question: How do you feel toward God most days? I know, most of us would probably say we respect or revere him, want to honor him or serve him, perhaps fear him. But do you *like* him?

IF YOU ARE FEELING . . .

But I love God. Yes, many of us have said that for years, almost automatically, "religiously." But loving someone and liking him are two different things, especially when you feel you *ought* to love him. Family is a good example. Or perhaps the people at church. We feel obligated to love them. But do you *like* them? Do you want to spend all your free time with them?

Think of the people in your life with whom you really do want to spend some time. Let's say you're taking a vacation and a few friends can come along. Make a list of people you would invite. Why? What is it about them that you enjoy?

When we try to identify what we like about people, we find that it's sometimes hard to put into words. It's not their *efficiency* (you probably wouldn't take your accountant on vacation with you). It's not their *knowledge* (I doubt you'd ask a professor to come along, just because he's smart). No, the people whose company we enjoy are those we enjoy *as people*. It's their personality—their heart—that we enjoy, isn't it? Of course. So, do you enjoy the personality of God? Has the thought ever crossed your mind that he *has* a personality, a heart?

TO CLARIFY

Melville said, "The reason the mass of men fear God, and at bottom dislike him, is because they rather distrust his heart, and fancy him all brain, like a watch."[33]

A watch was one of the more complex and mechanical objects of Melville's day. We might say "computer" instead. Many people see God that way, as the great computer brain behind the universe. Or like Christof, the director of *The Truman Show*, mentioned in the last chapter. The bottom line is, it's just not possible to love and trust someone whose heart we suspect.

FINDING THE HEART OF GOD

How can I trust a Lover who is so wild? "There's only one possible answer: You could love him if you *knew* his heart was good." And so we must search to find the heart of God. To do this, I said, we must see God not as the Author of the play but as the central character *in* it. Is that a new idea to you—that God has been playing a role *in* the story of life?

Name several of the heroes that you love, the characters at the center of your favorite stories. Then write down what it is about them that makes you love them, cheer for them, root for them.

WINDOW

As we mentioned earlier, the hero of the Chronicles of Narnia is a great and noble lion named Aslan. All the Narnians love him, and many readers of those tales have fallen in love with Aslan too. He's so good and kind, so brave and true.

In fact, a little boy once wrote C. S. Lewis a letter in which he confessed that he loved Aslan more than Jesus. Perhaps you can relate—if not through Aslan, then through another hero that you love. God doesn't seem nearly so close, so human, as they. In the song "Hero" (I quoted part of it in chapter 4), the refrain goes like this:

> And the reason that she loved him
> Was the reason I loved him too
> And he never wondered what was
> Right or wrong
> He just knew
> He just knew

Ever so wisely, Lewis wrote back and told the boy that all that he loved about Aslan *is* Jesus.[34]

ACT I: HIS ETERNAL HEART

Now we venture back to discover the story of God, to watch him, to try to look at things from his point of view as a character in the story. In particular, we want to know, "What is his motive? How does life affect him?" Prior to reading the chapter, when you thought about the Christian view of life's story, did you ever think about life *before* creation, before Eden?

All of us have at one time or another wished that we could have somebody else's life. (This is the whole fascination with *People* magazine and social media.) What kind of life do you think God gets to live? Would words such as *adventurous* and *intimate* and *exciting* come to mind? (Have you ever even thought about the kind of life God lives?)

And if you seldom think about God's life or his story, who does that leave in the center of the story you *do* think about?

"Our story begins with the hero in love." I confess that before writing *The Sacred Romance*, I had pretty much always thought of God as alone until he made mankind. Have you? How does it feel to know that from all eternity God has been loving and caring, that he has always been community, that the heart of the universe is perfect love?

As human beings, we long to know that love is real and will not go away. Children need to know they are loved, but even more, they need to know that their parents truly love *each other* because love then seems secure. This is the reason that divorce strikes children so deeply—because it ends the story of love. How does it strike you to know that you come from a circle of true love, from "the laughter of the Trinity"?

In this chapter, I described my experience on my grandfather's ranch; how wonderful it was that I could be invited up into a grand story that was already underway, one that I didn't have to start, but got to be a part of. Have you ever had an experience like that? (Boys often look for it in making the team, being given a position to play. Girls might get a taste of it when they are invited to the dance they've been longing to go to.) Have you ever been invited into something? How did it make you feel? And if you can't recall even one occasion, don't you *long* to be invited "in"?

TO CLARIFY

Eugene Peterson says, "Traditional Christian spirituality is not taking bits and pieces of doctrine and putting them to use, it's entering into the life of God that is already in motion. . . . A home that is ordered by Father, Son, and Holy Spirit."[35]

In other words, we need to know that before we arrived, something great had already been going on.

The best thing about the ranch was that "I wasn't responsible for it. It didn't depend on me." Aren't the best things in life like that? Surprise parties, pickup games, running into an old friend, spontaneous moments of joy? Does Christianity feel like that to you—like a wonderful invitation or surprise? Or does it feel like something you have to "get right" or "master," something that pretty much rests on your shoulders?

Thinking of you. Such simple words, found on many cards and letters, let us know that we are loved because we are remembered, we are in the thoughts of someone who might be far away. Though time and space separate us, how comforting to hear that we are not forgotten. Now listen to these words from Ephesians 1: "Long before he laid down earth's foundations, [God] had us in mind, had settled on us as the focus of his love, to be made whole and holy by his love. . . . Long before we first heard of Christ and got our hopes up, he had his eye on us, had designs on us for glorious living" (verses 4, 11–12 MSG). What is it like to consider that God has been thinking of you for a very, very long time?

ACT II: HIS HEART BETRAYED

Act II reveals that the story involves other characters. Angels are often depicted in movies, artwork, and even Valentine's Day cards. But somehow, they don't quite capture the majestic beings portrayed in Scripture. For example, how many angels did it take to destroy Sodom and Gomorrah (see Genesis 19:1)? How many angels will it take to destroy one-third of mankind (see Revelation 9:15)? Are these cute little babies with tiny wings?

What is the role of the holy angels today (see Hebrews 1:14)?

Have you ever wondered where evil came from? Did you suppose it started with the fall of man, in the Garden?

Notice something: Every great story has a villain. God's story does too. The problem is, we tend to ignore that fact and blame all the bad stuff on God or on ourselves. What difference would it make to know that there really *is* a villain and that God has to deal with him as much as we do?

Recall a recent event in which things did not go well. How did you think about it? Was the evil one even a consideration? What role, if any, do you allow for him?

TO CLARIFY

C. S. Lewis said there are two mistakes when dealing with the devil: to blame everything on him, or to blame nothing on him.[36] The church at present has fallen mostly to the second error. We don't live as if the story has a villain. And so we are deeply confused about many things that are happening.

Have you ever been betrayed? Have you ever had a group turn on you? What did it feel like? Do you think God felt something like that when his most beautiful angel—Lucifer—betrayed him and led many other angels to do the same?

IF YOU ARE FEELING . . .

Wow, that's a powerful story Milton told about the war in heaven! But is it biblical? *Indeed, it is.*

Genesis 3:1–4: Satan had obviously fallen by the time Adam and Eve were created because he was there to tempt them away from God.

Ezekiel 28:12–17: The motives of the evil one are exposed, and his fall described.

Revelation 12: Sometime in the past, there was a great angelic battle in heaven, which Satan lost.

There are two kinds of love—selfish love and generous love. Selfish love creates those closed systems we've all encountered, the cliques we've met at work or school or church. You can't get in, no matter how hard you try. Generous love *wants* to let others in. When we see the Trinity begin writing others into the story, what kind of love is being shown? Is God self-centered?

ACT III: HIS HEART ON TRIAL

Act III, which begins in Genesis, reveals our Hero as a sculptor, painter, artist. You can learn a lot about the soul of an artist from his work. For example, we know that Edgar Allan Poe must have been a tortured soul, given his dark and evil stories. We also know what a joyful and worshipful person Bach must have been for the most part, given his music. What can we learn about the heart of God through his creation? Take a walk through the woods or along the beach. Spend time in a garden. Or spend an hour looking at photos of beautiful and exotic places. What kind of person would make this symphony?

And how much beauty does he offer? "Gloriously wasteful, O my Lord, art thou!" proclaimed George MacDonald.[37] Sunset after sunset, flowers upon flowers, a thousand mysteries to be explored. And who was creation given *to*? Whose name is on this gift? Ours! Is our Hero generous?

Then God creates men and women, in his image. Now, we know God doesn't have a body, so we must bear his image in our *souls*. He gave us deep and rich and wondrous hearts, capable of loving and laughing and living. What does this tell us about *his* heart?

Then God gives us freedom. Why? What does this tell us about why we are here? Is it to serve God or to love him?

━━━━━━━━━━ TO CLARIFY ━━━━━━━━━━

The whole thing turns on the issue of love. If you want a world where love really matters, then you have to have a world where we have free will. Love is love only when it's freely chosen. And to give us free will, and not take it back when we misuse it, means that God has to take an enormous risk.

If you have been betrayed or turned against by an entire group, how did you respond? Did it take some time before you were willing to love again? Have you ever been quite as vulnerable afterward? What does it say about the heart of God that he chooses vulnerability over self-protection?

How have you understood the fall of man and woman? As a crime mostly, or as a betrayal of love? How do you suppose God experienced it? Did it hurt him? (See also Genesis 6:5–6.)

Even though we broke his heart, did he turn his back on us?

I call the Old Testament "the long story of God's pursuit of humanity." Have you looked at it that way before? How does it feel to know that God is the One pursuing you?

In the Prophets, the heart of God is revealed as nowhere else. What do we find there? Is it surprising to you to see God as a jealous lover?

═══════════════ **TO CLARIFY** ═══════════════

Theologians and Bible teachers have told many of us that God is "impassable," that he does not experience emotion as we humans do. Is that what you find when you read Isaiah or Jeremiah or Hosea? A. W. Tozer pleads in *The Pursuit of God*: "We have almost forgotten that God is a person . . . and in the deep of his mighty nature he thinks, wills, enjoys, feels, loves, desires and suffers as any other person may."[38]

In *Disappointment with God*, Phil Yancey tells of going to a cabin in the mountains in Colorado to face his doubts about God and to read the Bible for himself. What he discovered changed his life:

Simply reading the Bible, I encountered not a misty vapor but an actual Person. A Person as unique and distinctive and colorful as any person I know. God has deep emotions; he feels delight and frustration and anger . . . As I read through the Bible in my winter aerie, I marveled at how much God lets human beings affect him. I was unprepared for the joy and anguish—in short, the passion—of the God of the Universe. By studying "about" God, by taming him and reducing him to words and concepts that could be filed away in alphabetical order, I had lost the force of the passionate relationship God seeks above all else. The people who related to God best—Abraham, Moses, David, Isaiah, Jeremiah—treated him with startling familiarity. They talked to God as if he were sitting in a chair beside them, as one might talk to a counselor, a boss, a parent, or a lover. They treated him like a person.[39]

GOD TAKES ON THE HUMAN POINT OF VIEW

What was your reaction to Kierkegaard's parable of the king and the maiden? Have you ever seen the Incarnation that way?

WINDOW

In a beautiful song called "The Dance of the Bride," Julie Meyer sings of God's love for us:

Said the Bridegroom to the Bride
You are my Lover, my Joy and Pride
We'll be together side by side
So come away from dawn through the night in the dance

Said the Bridegroom to the Bride
I have loved you every day of your life
And it was destiny, not by chance
That I'm Lord of your heart and
Lord of your Dance

"The Incarnation, the life and death of Jesus, answers once and for all the question, 'What is God's heart toward me?' This is why Paul says in Romans 5, 'Look here, at the cross. Here is the demonstration of God's heart. At the point of our deepest betrayal, when we had run our farthest from him and gotten so lost in the woods we could never find our way home, God came and died to rescue us.' We don't have to wait for the Incarnation to see God as a character in the story and learn something of his motives. But after the coming of Jesus, there can be no doubt."

WINDOW

One of my all-time favorite movies is *Braveheart*. It is perhaps the most stunning picture of Christ that Hollywood has ever painted. After coming to fight for his homeland, William Wallace dies so that his people might be free. His execution is a terrifyingly beautiful scene, and it has impacted many Christians more deeply than the typical crucifixion stories. The film has quite a following, and I know why. Remember the little boy who loved Aslan? All that people have loved in Braveheart *is* Jesus.

How have you understood the death of Jesus? How have you interpreted what he did, *why* he came? Do you even think about it much?

Has anyone ever loved you like this? Have you ever been pursued by the very person you rejected?

─────────────── **WINDOW** ───────────────

I belong to my beloved,
   and his desire is for me. . . .
Place me like a seal over your heart,
   like a seal on your arm;
for love is as strong as death,
   its jealousy unyielding as the grave (Song of Songs 7:10; 8:6).

O help me, God, to see your heart for me. Take away all the dark things I have believed about you. Reveal to me your great heart. Through Christ I pray. Amen.

───

WINDOWS

Film

The Last of the Mohicans (Twentieth Century Fox, 1992). A dramatic story of romance set in a life-and-death battle.

Braveheart (Paramount Pictures, 1995). There's some strong stuff here, especially the battle scenes. Just close your eyes—the rest of the film is worth it. *Braveheart* has done for many of my students what none of the films about Jesus could do.

Music

Braveheart motion picture soundtrack (Decca Records, 1995). Especially tracks 1, 11, 17, and 18.

"Dance of the Bride" by Julie Meyer, from *You Make Me Smile* (Liber Music, 1998).

Books

Disappointment with God by Phil Yancey (Grand Rapids: Zondervan, 1988). I owe Yancey an enormous debt. He was one of the first to draw me to see the larger story and the heart of God revealed in it. This is a wonderful book.

Telling the Truth: The Gospel as Tragedy, Comedy, and Fairy Tale by Frederick Buechner (New York: Harper & Row, 1977).

7

THE BELOVED

I belong to my beloved, and his desire is for me.

SONG OF SONGS 7:10

YOUR INITIAL REACTION

In two or three minutes, jot down the things that struck you when you read this chapter. What were your initial thoughts, emotions, impressions?

I felt . . .

I realized . . .

I wanted . . .

PRAYER OF BEGINNING

When I consider your heavens,
the work of your fingers,
the moon and the stars,
which you have set in place,
what is mankind that you are mindful of them,
human beings that you care for them? (Psalm 8:3-4).

Dear Jesus, who am I really? What do you see in me that you would move heaven and earth to capture my heart? My life feels like a collection of other people's expectations and disappointments. I do not even know anymore who I truly am. Reveal to me my true identity, my true place in your story. Give me grace to hear your voice; shut out all other voices, and let me hear from you alone. I ask this in your name. Amen.

TO CLARIFY

Here are the central truths of this chapter:

- Next to what we think of God, what we think of ourselves is our most important belief.
- We learn who we are from others, from the impact we have had on them.
- This means, for most of us, that we have created a "false self," which we hide behind.
- But when we see the impact we've had on God, the role he has given us in his story, we see that we truly are the Beloved.

WHO AM I?

Chapter 7 explores how we think about ourselves and our role in the story. This is no small matter. Next to what we believe about God, what we believe about ourselves is our most important belief. As I wrote in this chapter, "There is no escaping your identity. You will not live beyond how you see yourself; not for long." Deep in our heart there lies another question: Who *am* I really?

To begin with, take a few minutes and write a description of how you see yourself. Specifically *what is it about you that would make others grateful for you?* Why would someone want you?

Was it hard to think of anything? If you came up with a few things, are they more about what you can *do* or who you *are*? Can you see the difference?

WINDOW

Walter Mitty, the main character of *The Secret Life of Walter Mitty*, is an employee at *LIFE* magazine who spends day after monotonous day developing photos for publication. To escape the tedium, he inhabits a world of daydreams filled with adventure. But when the prized cover photo for the final issue goes missing, he is suddenly forced into the world of real-life adventure as he travels to Greenland and the Himalayas to track down the reclusive photographer. Walter is transformed by the experience and finds a source of courage within that he didn't know he possessed. The movie is a great story of what can happen when you discover your true identity and embrace the life God created you for.

OUR DOUBLE BIND

We want to be known, and we fear it like nothing else. We want to be known because we are made in the image of the Trinity, the relational God. We want to be known because we were made for intimacy. So let me ask you a basic question: How known do you feel in your life right now? Does anyone pay real attention to you, and if you do receive attention, why?

Can you name the people in your life currently who have really taken the time to get to know you, your deep heart? Are there more or less of them than in years gone by?

—— LISTEN TO ——
YOUR HEART

Don't you want to be
really and truly known by
at least somebody?

Have you ever felt really special to someone? When? Why?

We long for intimacy, but we also fear it because of the Fall. We know we are not what we were meant to be. Where in your life, and with whom, do you feel free to let all the guards down and just be yourself? How often can you allow yourself such freedom?

If you were to sit down with the key people in your life, one at a time, and ask what you are like to live with, what do you secretly fear they will say? How do you like that suggestion?

THE CREATION OF THE FALSE SELF

We learn who we are from others. That's one of the deep truths of this chapter. We are made for community, and it is in community, in relationship, that we develop our sense of self. "We come into the world with a longing to be known and a deep-seated fear that we aren't what we should be. We are set up for a crisis of identity.... And then, says Frederick Buechner... 'the world sets in to making us what the world would like us to be, and because we have to survive after all, we try to make ourselves into something that we hope the world will like better than it apparently did the selves we originally were.'"[40]

Back in chapter 1, we said that starting at a very young age, life teaches us to ignore our hearts. Quite often we learn from parents and peers, from teachers and spiritual leaders, that the life of the heart is not worth living. We learn from the key people in our lives that "efficiency and performance are everything." Think about the people you looked up to as a child. What did they want from you? What did they expect you to be? What "role" did they assume you would play? The good girl? The athlete? The straight-A student? The wealthy doctor?

Parents

Friends

Teachers

Church leaders

I said in this chapter that because of the story of our life, we all learn at some level to offer something functional to win the approval of others and avoid their contempt. These are the "coats and hats" that Buechner refers to, the selves we learn to put on. Is that a new thought to you—that your personality is not wholly God-given but something that has been shaped and, furthermore, has a *purpose* behind it?

In the story of your life, what has earned you praise?

How much do you rely on it today?

In the story of your life, what has earned you ridicule, scorn, or worse?

How much do you try to avoid it today?

Put those two together and you've got the "false self," the person you are trying to be to get a little love and avoid rejection. But as I said, "The awful burden of the false self is that it must be constantly maintained." What do you feel that you *have* to be in the various roles of your life?

At home

At work

At church

TO CLARIFY

One woman told me through tears, "It's probably service. I'm known as a real servant. But you see, if I'm needed, then I'm okay. What would I offer if I didn't serve? Who would I be?"

A thought that has never occurred to most of us is this: "Your evaluation of your soul . . . is probably wrong." It's probably wrong because it comes from a world filled with people still terribly confused about who *they* are. Has it ever struck you that the world might have been wrong about you?

LISTEN TO
YOUR HEART

Do you like the pressure of maintaining the false self? Wouldn't you love to give all that up? Wouldn't you love to be free to be yourself—without fear?

OUR IMPACT ON GOD

"Identity is not something that falls on us out of the sky. For better or for worse, identity is *bestowed*." We will draw our sense of self from others. That's just the way it will always be. So the question is, *From whom?* From the person who loves us most, the person on whom we've had the greatest impact. Let's look again at the impact we have had on God.

God creates us to live in his love. Our rejection of him breaks his heart. Still, he does not reject us. He sent his prophets to call us back to his heart. Finally, he sent his only Son to die for us, to free us from the prisons of darkness and make us his own once more. God came at a great price to rescue us. He made a daring raid into enemy territory just to win us back. Is that a new thought to you? What is it like for you to think that it may be true?

Given the way God acts, do you think that he *desires* you?

TO CLARIFY

Remember that there's a difference between loving someone and liking him. We've heard a thousand times that God loves us. But does God *like* you? Not everything you do, but *you*?

In the last chapter, we talked about the fact that those we want to spend our time with are those whose hearts we enjoy. Does God want to spend his time with you? Reconsider the story of Martha and Mary (see Luke 10:38-42).

Is God thinking about you? Read Psalm 139:17–18. How often is God thinking about you? What do you suppose he's thinking about as he thinks of you?

——— LISTEN TO ——— YOUR HEART

Many, many people assume that God is disappointed when he thinks about them. Do you? Where did that thought come from?

God has been pursuing us from farther away than space and longer ago than time. That's the astounding message of the Sacred Romance. The question each of us naturally asks is, *Why?* What does he want from me? We've been offered many explanations: obedience, sacrifice, adherence to doctrine, and so on. What do you think? Who told you that?

In the face of every other answer the world and the church have tried to give us, I believe the only real answer is this: "What he is after is *us*—our laughter, our tears, our dreams, our fears, our heart of hearts." How does that thought make you feel? Do you think it's true? What if it *were* true?

What would it take to convince you it is true?

The Pharisees had their act together in every way—religiously, socially, spiritually. They were doing all the right things, keeping the law as best a person could. Yet Jesus was saddened by them, for he said, "These people honor me with their lips, but their *hearts* are far from me" (Matthew 15:8, emphasis added). So, what does God want more than anything else from his people?

WHO WE ARE TO GOD

In the chapter, I suggest a number of ascending metaphors, each one more significant than the other, that Scripture uses to describe our relationship with God. Which of these best describes your relationship with God from your point of view? Where do you put yourself? Why there?

Lover   Beloved

Friend   Friend

Father   Child

Master   Servant

Shepherd   Sheep

But aren't we *sinners*? Yes, every one of us has fallen; we've all turned our backs on God, time and time again. But I'm very concerned about how you hear that word, *sinners*. Are we pond scum or glorious ruins? Did we start out as sinners? Do we end that way?

═══ WINDOW ═══

In the 1998 film *Les Misérables*, there is a woman who falls into a life of prostitution because of tragedy and financial ruin. Her name is Fantine. The hero, Jean Valjean, rescues her from an assault and imprisonment and takes her to his home where she can be cared for.

> VALJEAN: You need to rest.
>
> FANTINE: You don't want to kiss?
>
> VALJEAN: I want you to rest. And don't worry. I'll bring your daughter to you . . . She will attend the school and you won't have any more worries. When you're better, I'll find work for you.
>
> FANTINE: But you don't understand. I'm a whore. And [my daughter] has no father.
>
> VALJEAN: She has the Lord. He is her father. And you're his creation. In his eyes, you've never been anything but an innocent and beautiful woman.

TO CLARIFY

Neil Anderson has pointed out that most Christians see themselves as "forgiven sinners." But that's not how the Bible describes a Christian. Salvation *transforms* us; makes us into new creations. You are not a sinner but a saint who sometimes sins. Here is a sampling of verses that describe your new identity:

> You are a new creation (2 Corinthians 5:17).
> You are a saint (Ephesians 1:1).
> You are holy and dearly loved (Colossians 3:12).
> You are no longer darkness but now are light in the Lord (Ephesians 5:8).
> You are united with Christ (1 Corinthians 6:17).
> You are God's Beloved (Romans 1:7).[41]

I believe that as hard as it is to admit and face our sin, it is harder still for us to see our "glory," our true self that is not evil but glorious. Why do you think that is?

Our sin gives us something to work on, something to be fixed so that then we are lovable. But our glory is beyond any fixing—it's just who we are. What might be desirable in you that God moved heaven and earth to get?

Dare we ask him? But we must. To truly embrace our part in the story, we've got to get our self-perception healed. We must hear from the One who knows. I want you to do something: Ask him. Ask God what he thinks of you. And don't just ask him once; keep on asking him till you are able to hear his answer.

A WARNING

The voice of God is never condemning (see Romans 8:1). The evil one condemns us; distorts our view of God and ourselves. God will never say anything to you that contradicts what he says about you in Scripture (that you are a saint, his Beloved, holy and dearly loved).

But we must also hear his *personal* word to us. So ask him. Make sure you write down what you hear over the next few days and weeks.

WINDOW

God speaks to us through Scripture, of course. But often he speaks to us through other means, such as his creation, and through art and music. In fact, the Sacred Romance is everywhere. Listen to God's heart as expressed through Dan Fogelberg's song "Longer":

Longer than there've been fishes in the ocean
Higher than any bird ever flew
Longer than there've been stars up in the heavens
I've been in love with you.

Stronger than any mountain cathedral
Truer than any tree ever grew
Deeper than any forest primeval
I am in love with you.

God wants to be your Lover. Would you like him to be?

Let's look again at Ephesians 1:4, 11–12. Paul makes it clear that we've been more than noticed: "Long before he laid down earth's foundations, he had us in mind, had settled on us as the focus of his love, to be made whole and holy by his love . . . Long before we first heard of Christ and got our hopes up, he had his eye on us, had designs on us for glorious living" (MSG).

If there isn't anything we have to do to earn his love, if we're not under pressure to continually maintain a false self so that he will like us, what might you be released from having to keep up personally? What about your false self might you be able to let go?

WINDOWS

Film

The Secret Life of Walter Mitty (20th Century Fox, 2013). This edition of the film, starring Ben Stiller and Kristen Wiig, is an adaptation of a 1939 short story of the same name by James Thurber. Portions of the film were shot in Iceland, which provide some stunning visuals.

Les Misérables (Columbia/TriStar, 1998). A very, very powerful picture of the gospel in film.

Music
"Longer" by Dan Fogelberg, from *Phoenix* (Epic Records, 1979).

Books
Abba's Child by Brennan Manning (Colorado Springs, CO: NavPress, 1994). Subtitled *The Cry of the Heart for Intimate Belonging*. Manning beautifully reveals our false self and leads us in the way of the true self as God's Beloved.

8

THE ADVERSARY: LEGENDS OF THE FALL

The great snake lies ever half awake, at the bottom of the pit of the world, until he awakens in hunger.

T. S. ELIOT[42]

YOUR INITIAL REACTION

In two or three minutes, jot down the things that struck you when you read this chapter. What were your initial thoughts, emotions, impressions?

I felt . . .

I realized . . .

I wanted . . .

PRAYER OF BEGINNING

Keep me as the apple of your eye;
hide me in the shadow of your wings
from the wicked who are out to destroy me,
from my mortal enemies who surround me (Psalm 17:8-9).

Dear Jesus, open my eyes to the truth of the enemy who stalks me. Let me not be ignorant of his ploys, my head buried in the sand. Neither let me be afraid, intimidated by the one you have beaten. Expose the adversary's work in my life and break the power of his lies. Show me your triumph and my secure place in you. I ask this in your name. Amen.

TO CLARIFY

Here are the central truths of this chapter:

- God has a mortal enemy, and so do you.
- His motive is to hurt God by hurting us.
- His strategy is to ruin the Sacred Romance by taking our hearts out of the picture through intimidation or seduction.
- But if we will live with our eyes open, his ploys merely take us deeper into God and the Sacred Romance.

THERE'S AN ENEMY?

Let's come back to the basic elements of every story: character, plot, and setting. When we are mistaken about any one of these three, we will be very, very confused about the story unfolding around us. For example, think of the classic *The Wizard of Oz*. When Dorothy wakes up from the tornado, she finds she is not in Kansas anymore. The setting has changed, and she must adjust to it. No longer can she live as though she was still on the farm.

The plot has changed as well; life has become a dangerous journey to find her way home. How foolish she would be to ignore her new situation. For one thing, she would never find the Emerald City, never find her way home. But a worse fate might befall her, for the *characters* have changed. The Wicked Witch of the West is after her, and Dorothy must live as though she has a mortal enemy or her naïveté will hurt her—badly.

How clear are you on the plot, characters, and setting of the Sacred Romance, the drama unfolding all around you? What role have you understood the adversary to play in the world and in life generally?

And what about in *your* life specifically?

The apostle Paul wrote to the believers at Corinth to warn them not to be outwitted by the enemy, for, as he said, "We are not ignorant of his schemes" (2 Corinthians 2:11 NASB). In what ways do you feel prepared to resist your enemy? Or, like many of us, are you mostly ignorant of his schemes? Why is that?

If you knew, for example, there was a mugger who sometimes visited your neighborhood, how would you act differently? What precautions would you take?

IF YOU ARE FEELING . . .

I don't want to deal with this. It scares me. Many believers feel that way. But there is no reason to be afraid: "For God has not given us a spirit of fear and timidity, but of power, love, and self-discipline" (2 Timothy 1:7 NLT). You are about to learn how safe you truly are.

However, if you choose to ignore your enemy, you will make yourself even *more* vulnerable to his attacks. Do you think he goes away just because you pull the covers over your head? "*Resist* the devil," the Bible says, "and he will flee from you" (James 4:7, emphasis added).

THE PLOT

We are in the midst of a battle. Scripture vividly depicts us as in a world at war. And the battle is actually in our hearts or, better, *for* our hearts. As Brent wrote, "The journey of our individual hearts, as well as the heart of an entire nation or culture, really distills into this warfare for our heart's devotion. It is the central plot of the Sacred Romance, Act III, life here on earth. Indeed, all of the subplots of our lives come out of it." So, what is the real plot of *your* story now? What is at stake, and who is fighting whom for it?

Very, very few Christians live as though we are at war. How would you say that most Christians do live? What movie do they think we're in? And why is that, do you suppose?

WINDOW

In his book *D-Day*, historian Stephen Ambrose gives a stunning account of the climactic battle of World War II and the men who waged the most daring of all invasions. On the night before the Allies hit the beaches at Normandy, the 82nd and 101st Airborne Divisions were dropped in behind enemy lines to begin the invasion and cut off Hitler's reinforcements. It was a moment of unparalleled bravery . . . and cowardice. For not every paratrooper played the man that fateful night.

> Too many had hunkered down in hedgerows to await the dawn; a few had even gone to sleep. Pvt. Francis Palys of the 506th saw what was perhaps the worst dereliction of duty. He had gathered a squad near Vierville. Hearing "all kinds of noise and singing from a distance," he and his men sneaked up on a farmhouse. In it was a mixed group from both American divisions. The paratroopers had found [liquor] in the cellar . . . and "they were drunker than a bunch of hillbillies on a Saturday night wingding. Unbelievable."[43]

Unbelievable indeed. The men knew they were at war, yet they refused to act like it. And their refusal endangered them and countless others. A *very* sobering picture of the church in America. We simply do not act as though we are at war.

SATAN'S DEFEAT

Before we more carefully expose the work of the evil one in our lives, I want to re-move any fears you may have. Satan has been defeated. Think again about your favorite stories. The best ones reach a climax where the villain is defeated and the heroes live "happily ever after." I love it when the Wicked Witch of the West gets a bucket of water in the face and melts away, to everyone's astonishment. Or when the evil queen in *Sleeping Beauty*—revealed to be a dragon after all—gets a sword through the heart. Why do we cheer when the villain goes down?

Now take a careful look at the following Scriptures:

1 John 3:8: According to this passage, why did Christ come?

John 12:31: And what did Jesus say would happen to the devil?

Hebrews 2:14–15: Did it happen?

Colossians 2:13–15: What happened to all of Satan's evil forces at the cross?

Ephesians 1:18–23: After the Resurrection, what happened for Jesus, and what happened to the forces of evil?

Matthew 28:18: How far does the authority of Jesus Christ now extend?

Colossians 1:13: And what has God done for you?

Ephesians 2:6: What sort of position of authority do you have now?

Luke 10:19: How much authority has Jesus given you over the devil?

TO CLARIFY

If Satan has been defeated, why even think about him?

Though he has been disarmed, the day of his final destruction has not yet come. According to the book of Revelation, in the meantime, "woe to the earth and the sea, because the devil has gone down to you! He is filled with fury, because he knows that his time is short" (12:12). Peter warned us, "Be alert and of sober mind. Your enemy the devil prowls around like a roaring lion looking for someone to devour" (1 Peter 5:8). The battle is not over yet!

A HEART FOR REVENGE

What is Satan's basic motive? Whom is he ultimately trying to hurt, and whom does he go after?

Recall the stories you love and the villains you hate. Name the worst. What can you learn from his motives, the way he operates?

══════════════ **WINDOW** ══════════════

Amadeus is a fictional account in film of the life and death of the famous composer Wolfgang Amadeus Mozart. His enemy, and murderer, is the court composer Salieri, whose heart is filled with jealousy when he realizes that Mozart's skill, beauty, and perfection are greater than his own. Reading Mozart's handwritten symphonies, he says, "Here was the very voice of God." Salieri storms out of the room, and in the privacy of his chambers he declares war on God. As he takes down the crucifix hanging on his bedroom wall and places it in the fire, he vows, "From now on, we are enemies—You and I. Because You choose for Your instrument [Mozart], and give me only the ability to recognize his greatness. Therefore I will block You, I swear it. I will hurt and harm Your incarnation on earth as far as I am able."

SATAN'S GRAND STRATEGY

Brent says that "God and Satan each have a design, a battle plan, to capture our heart's devotion." As you look over that passage again in the book, what is God's plan?

And what is Satan's plan?

How has Satan been disconnecting you from your heart, and from the heart of God?

"Part of Satan's grand strategy of separating us from our heart . . . is to convince us that our heart's desires are still *at core* illegitimate." What desires in your heart has Satan mocked and accused and condemned over the years? Or maybe it is better to ask, what desires have you felt were stupid, bad, or embarrassing?

And what have you done with those desires?

Can you relate to the story of Cinderella, the way the stepsisters' voices controlled her and kept her beaten down? Think about how this plays out in the lives of your loved ones (it's often easier to see this when it's not your life). Are they living with complete freedom of heart, confident of who they are to God? How has Satan whispered to them? What are their "stepsisters' voices"?

Now think about your life. What are the words and sentences that have kept you in the cellar? It might be helpful to consider a recent event where you failed or did something you regret. What were the sentences you heard afterward? Did you assume they came from your heart?

———— **LISTEN TO** ————
YOUR HEART

The next time something
bad happens, listen to the
voices within. What are
they saying about you?

Brent says, "The voice (sometimes voices) that accuses us is so familiar we have learned to think of it as our own." That's Satan's basic ploy—to get us to believe that he's not really there, that these things we struggle with are just our own mess. "He accuses us through the words of parents and friends and God himself." Is that a new thought to you—that it is really Satan behind all those accusations and Arrows? How does it change the way you see them, respond to them?

Not only does Satan accuse us, but he also accuses God *to* us; he uses the events of our lives to sow seeds of doubt in our hearts about God's goodness, his trustworthiness, and his love for us. Can you see this in your life? Think of a difficult or tragic event you've endured. What were the thoughts that went through your head about God?

LISTEN TO YOUR HEART

And the next time something bad happens, listen to the voices inside. What are they saying about God?

TO CLARIFY

A friend spent a quiet evening with his wife, the two of them reading in their family room. Now and then they would put down their books and share a few words. "I don't know why," he recalled to me later, "but every time she spoke to me I felt so *accused*. She wasn't saying anything condemning at all. Still, it felt that way."

Do you really think there were only two of them in the room?

If we do not live with a very keen awareness of the enemy, then we will blame ourselves, God, or others for an incredible amount of junk (I'm using a word my publisher will print). Satan is constantly putting his spin on things.

A DISGUISED ROAR

Using the dialogue from *Paradise Lost*, Brent shows us how Satan's basic plan is to try to seduce our hearts away from God or, if that fails, to "drive" us with fear and intimidation. What are the ways that Satan tempts you? How has he tried to seduce your heart over the years? Recently?

Where do you feel intimidated in your life? Where has fear gotten the best of you? Is it the fear of what others think of you? The fear of failure? The fear that your heart is not good, that you should never venture out into the fields of freedom but stay in the cellar of duty and obligation?

Satan is constantly stealing the true story from us. Brent spoke of how the enemy used the Arrows of his life to shape a story line designed to keep him in fear all his life. "You are on your own. There is no one to fall back on. . . . It's all going to end badly." What is the story line you fear is true about your life?

Can you begin to see how your enemy wrote it?

WINDOW

The King's Speech is a historical drama about George VI of England and a speech therapist named Lionel Logue. "Bertie," as he is known by his family, has coped with a stammer throughout his life. When he is suddenly thrust into the role of king—a position that requires him to give speeches to the nation—his wife calls on the services of Lionel for help. In their first session, Lionel has Bertie recite a few lines from *Hamlet* while listening to classic music played on a pair of headphones. Bertie is frustrated at the experiment, but Lionel gives him an acetate recording as a souvenir. When Bertie plays the recording later that night, he is astonished to discover that he read the lines without a stutter. Bertie realizes that his stuttering can be overcome and returns to Lionel for daily therapy sessions. In the same way, Satan tries to get us to believe lies about ourselves and keep us from stepping into our roles. But God, like Lionel in the film, shows us that we have greater potential than we may realize.

"Satan's . . . lifelong purpose with each of us is to make sure we never know who we really are; indeed, to keep us living the life of a cellar maid rather than a princess." Notice how recently he has done this in your life. Did anything give you hope from the last chapter, "The Beloved"? Was there anything that lifted your heart as you read it and worked through the exercises? Is that "lift" of heart still with you today? If not, where did it go?

Does anything stir in your heart when you realize that you're not just forgetful but that these precious truths are being *stolen* from you? What does it move you to do?

The bottom line is, Satan works to tell us our desires are not good and there's no story that our desires are really for. How has that happened, even in your Christian life?

"As long as we do not admit that the deep things of our heart are there—the rejection and hurt, the shame and sorrow, the anger and rage—these rooms of our heart become darkened and the enemy sets up shop there to accuse us." Are there any rooms in your heart you suspect need a good cleaning? This is the vital place for confession, repentance, and healing. When we bring our hearts openly and freely to God, seeking his cleansing, we are cleansed (see 1 John 1:8–9). And the evil one no longer gets to operate there.

WINDOW

In a song written by Rich Mullins simply titled "Jesus," Ashley Cleveland sings:

> Jesus, they drove the cold nails through your tired hands
> And rolled a stone to seal your grave
> Feels like the devil's rolled a stone onto my heart
> Can you roll that stone away?

We experience spiritual warfare more than we know; but because the enemy is a deceiver, we rarely detect it until the skirmish is over and we are left dazed and confused, wondering what hit us. Let me suggest a quick inventory. On a scale of 1 to 10 (with 10 being the highest), rate your life on these indicators:

___ I enjoy reading Scripture and get a great deal out of it.
___ I'm experiencing a deeper intimacy with God.
___ Prayer is something I look forward to and enjoy with little distraction.
___ I rejoice in who God made me.
___ I rarely feel condemnation.
___ Worship is something that flows easily for me.
___ I look forward to the future with hope and anticipation.

None of these are a sure sign of a healthy life in itself, and we all go through dry spells, but if your answers are consistently below 6, you may be under a cloud of oppression and not recognize it.[44] Perhaps the key point of this chapter is that "we do not experience the story of our lives on . . . neutral ground." We are at war, the war is over our hearts, and the enemy is doing everything he can to destroy the Sacred Romance for us. How will you live differently knowing this is true?

WHY DOES GOD ALLOW IT?

So why does God allow the evil one so much latitude? Why doesn't Jesus just get rid of him? As Brent pointed out, spiritual warfare is no picnic: "Sometimes there is a great price to be paid in the establishing of the kingdom of God in our heart and in the heavenlies." What is God up to? There are at least two reasons given to us in the Scriptures for why God permits the battle to rage, sometimes fiercely.

First, as Brent said, it deepens our communion with God. Paul spoke of his thorn in the flesh, "a messenger of Satan, to torment me. Three times I pleaded with the Lord to take it away from me. But he said to me, 'My grace is sufficient for you, for my power is made perfect in weakness'" (2 Corinthians 12:7–9). In other words, Paul's battle required him to depend on God's grace. How might your struggles actually be drawing you to a deeper place with God? Might you respond differently to them if you saw this deeper purpose? Do you want to pray harder, hold to the truth more firmly?

Second, we are in preparation: "Praise be to the LORD my Rock, who trains my hands for war, my fingers for battle" (Psalm 144:1). Jesus showed his disciples how to use his authority against the kingdom of darkness, and then he sent them out to give it a try. They came back with the report: "Lord, even the demons submit to us in your name" (Luke 10:17). If you looked at the battles you are facing as spiritual *development*, what would change in your attitude and approach to them?

HOW TO RESPOND

Reading the stories from *D-Day*, I am struck by the parallels to spiritual warfare. The men who hunkered down on the beach in fear, hoping to find some cover from the battle—they are the ones who did not survive. The ones who finally said, "Look, we're going to get shot at either way—we might as well fight back," are the ones who prevailed. *Resist* the devil, Scripture says, and he will flee from you.

Read Ephesians 6:10–18. What has God provided for our protection? How are we to use it?

Now read Luke 4:1–13, the description of how Jesus faced the devil in the wilderness. How did Jesus respond to the enemy's lies?

Finally, read Revelation 12:7–12. How do the saints ("our brothers and sisters") overcome Satan? What two weapons are used?

These are just a few examples of how Scripture teaches us to "resist." We put on the armor—daily. We fight back with the truth—Scripture. And we claim the blood of Christ against our enemy—anytime we encounter him.

═══ WINDOW ═══

Whoever dwells in the shelter of the Most High
will rest in the shadow of the Almighty.
I will say of the LORD, "He is my refuge and my fortress,
my God, in whom I trust."
Surely he will save you
from the fowler's snare
and from the deadly pestilence.
He will cover you with his feathers
and under his wings you will find refuge;
his faithfulness will be your shield and rampart.
You will not fear the terror of night,
nor the arrow that flies by day,
nor the pestilence that stalks in the darkness,
nor the plague that destroys at midday.
A thousand may fall at your side,
ten thousand at your right hand,
but it will not come near you.
You will only observe with your eyes
and see the punishment of the wicked.
If you say, "The LORD is my refuge,"
and you make the Most High your dwelling,
no harm will overtake you,
no disaster will come near your tent.
For he will command his angels concerning you
to guard you in all your ways (Psalm 91:1-11).

WINDOWS

Film

Amadeus (Warner, 1984). Peter Shaffer's fictional account of the life and untimely death of Mozart.

The King's Speech (Paramount Pictures, 2010).

Music
"Jesus" by Rich Mullins, from *The Jesus Record* (Myrrh Records, 1998).

Books
Victory Over the Darkness by Neil Anderson (Ventura, CA: Regal Books, 1997).

The Bondage Breaker by Neil Anderson (Eugene, OR: Harvest House, 1990).

9

LESS-WILD LOVERS

It is the nature of desire not to be satisfied, and most men live only for the gratification of it.

ARISTOTLE[45]

YOUR INITIAL REACTION

In two or three minutes, jot down the things that struck you when you read this chapter. What were your initial thoughts, emotions, impressions?

I felt . . .

I realized . . .

I wanted . . .

PRAYER OF BEGINNING

Create in me a pure heart, O God (Psalm 51:10).

Dear Jesus, it's true. I have taken other lovers to me, given my heart to them. Search me, God, and know my heart. Free me from the bonds of my own making, these "affairs" I have fallen into. For I cannot save myself or set my own heart free. I am at your mercy. Deliver me, and let me find again the path of life. In your name I pray. Amen.

TO CLARIFY

Here are the central truths of this chapter:

- Somewhere along the road, we leave our shimmering heart behind and try to live from duty and resignation.
- But it does not work; we cannot suppress desire forever.
- So we take to ourselves other lovers, less wild than God, who offer us a taste of life.
- It is only on the road less traveled—the way of the thirsty heart—that we can recover our journey again.

BEING HAUNTED

Chapter 9 makes an assumption about every person's spiritual life: "A deeper work in our heart is called for if we are to be able to continue our spiritual journey." No doubt that is why you picked up this workbook in the first place. But I'm curious. Do you have a much clearer sense now of what that deeper work is for *your* heart? Can you put some words to it?

Let's come back to the plot of the story: Life is a fierce battle for our hearts, for what Buechner called the "shimmering self" and what Brent describes as the "shining part of ourselves." This is the deepest place within us, what Proverbs 4:23 describes as "the springs of life" within (NASB). How is that part of you doing at this point in the journey?

We often experience that elusive heart within us as a "Haunting." Brent quotes Norman MacLean, who at the end of his life found himself "haunted by waters." What are you haunted by these days? Does anything call to your deep heart? A place you long to visit perhaps? Or a person? Music you find yourself returning to again and again? A yearning you can't quite put words to?

Sometimes the Haunting returns to us as a bittersweet ache. In the still hours of the night, what do you ache for?

RESIGNATION

"However the Haunting comes, it often brings with it a bittersweet poignancy of ache, the sense that we stood at a crossroads somewhere in the past and chose a turning that left some shining part of ourselves—perhaps the best part—behind, left it behind with the passion of youthful love, or the calling of a heart voca-tion, or simply in the sigh of coming to terms with the mundane requirements of life." Can you recall that crossroads in your heart's past? When did it occur? What happened? What did you leave behind?

When we are Haunted, we sense that *life is still out there on the road somewhere ahead of us*. How much anticipation would you say you live with these days? For what?

—— LISTEN TO ——
YOUR HEART

When you wake up first thing in the morning, what are you thinking about, looking forward to?

At some point, all of us take that shining something and push it to an abiding place called resignation. Resignation is accepting the loss of the Romance and the Haunting as final. *Oh, maybe it's true for others, the lucky few. But it's not true for me.* "It is the condition in which we choose to see good as no longer startling in its beauty and boldness, but simply as 'nice.' Evil is no longer surprising; it's normal." Are you captured by the beauty of goodness these days? How much evil does it take to shock you?

TWO HIGHWAYS

"Most of us are aware that the Christian life requires a pilgrimage of some sort. We know we are sojourners. What we have sometimes not given much thought to is what kind of journey we are to be taking." In the exercises for chapter 1, I asked you to describe or define the Christian life. Take a look at your answer. How does it compare to Brent's imagery of a journey?

In this chapter, Brent writes of two very different "highways" from which we all choose on our spiritual journey. Describe both. What qualities make them different?

Which highway would you say you have been on the past several years? Have you changed from one to the other?

Think of people you secretly admire, people whose lives you wish you had. Which road have they chosen?

The dilemma with the "straight highway of discipline and duty" is that it eventually leads us right back to resignation. "We find ourselves struggling to weep with those who weep or even rejoice with those who rejoice. Mostly we don't bother looking people in the eye. They may want to engage us and nothing much inside feels very engaged. Our passions begin to show up in inappropriate fantasies and longings interspersed with depression, anxieties, and anger we thought we had left behind." What part of that condition rings true for you?

LIFE IN VANITY FAIR

If we leave the shimmering self (our deep heart) behind and give up on the Romance for a life that feels safer, our desire does not go away. "Our heart will not totally forsake the intimacy and adventure we were made for and so we compromise. We both become, and take to ourselves, 'lovers' . . . that are less wild." Why "less-wild" lovers?

Brent puts our less-wild lovers (and us, who become less-wild lovers) into basically two groups. What are they, and which one do you think you fall into more often than not?

People in the first group choose to deaden their hearts through *competence* or *order*. Do you know people like this? Are you one? What describes this lifestyle?

WINDOW

In the movie *The Accidental Tourist*, William Hurt plays a man who has lost heart because of a major Arrow—the death of his son. He lives in resignation, his whole life committed to controlling anything that might be remotely wild or even unfamiliar. He makes his living writing travel guidebooks called *The Armchair Traveler*, where he teaches middle-class American businessmen how to insulate themselves as they travel the world. Paris can feel just like Cleveland, as if you never left home. What happens in his redemption makes for a beautiful story.

Certain emotions can become less-wild lovers, "particularly shame, fear, lust, anger, and false guilt. They are emotions that 'protect' us from the more dangerous feelings of grief, abandonment, disappointment, loneliness, and even joy and longing, that threaten to roam free in the wilder environs of the heart." Where do you usually "live" emotionally? In other words, what emotions do you most often allow yourself to feel? And what does that protect you from feeling? What do you rarely, if ever, allow yourself to feel?

The people in the second group of less-wild lovers choose *indulgence* as their means of deadening their hearts. Do you know people like this? Are you one? What describes this lifestyle?

WINDOW

In his song "The Needle and the Damage Done," Neil Young describes the cycle of a drug addiction and then explains how he sees it in all of us:

I caught you knockin' at my cellar door
I love you, baby, can I have some more
Oh, oh, the damage done.
I hit the city and I lost my band
I watched the needle take another man
Gone, gone, the damage done.
I've seen the needle and the damage done
A little part of it in everyone.

Indulgence is a dangerous choice because once we give our heart to a less-wild lover, "it attaches itself to our desire with chains that render us captive." Have you tried to give up something you knew might be an addiction? Was it possible?

TO CLARIFY

Addiction psychologist Gerald May says in *Addiction and Grace* that repressing our desire is not as dangerous as attaching it to things: "While repression stifles desire, addiction *attaches* desire, bonds and enslaves the energy of desire to certain specific behaviors, things, or people. These objects of attachment then become preoccupations and obsessions; they come to rule our lives."[46]

If our deepest longings are for intimacy (for love or a sense of security) and adventure (or meaning, a sense of significance), then where do *you* go these days for a taste of each? (Men often focus on adventure and choose lovers such as sports. Women focus on intimacy, turning to soap operas or romance novels.)

LISTEN TO YOUR HEART

If I told you that you had to give up one of your deepest pleasures, which would cause you the most pain to let go of?

IF YOU ARE FEELING . . .

To be honest, I'm not sure what my "less-wild lovers" are. You aren't alone in feeling this, especially if you've chosen control and duty and efficiency, because they don't look like addictions.

Spend twenty minutes alone, in silence. Don't pray, read, or do anything. Just sit there. What comes chattering to your heart? What are you pulled to do, plan, dream about, or worry about? There are your other lovers.

In *Addiction and Grace*, May explains that every addiction shares five similar qualities, or stages: (1) tolerance, (2) withdrawal symptoms, (3) self-deception, (4) loss of willpower, and (5) distortion of attention. The following questions (adapted from May's work) may help you to see where your heart is attached to other lovers. First, here are questions that may reveal *tolerance* (growing to need something, becoming attached to it):

- Do you feel that you have enough in your life right now—enough money, enough of a favorite pastime—or do you feel you'd really be better off with more?
- Are you content with your status at work or at home? Is your sense of power and control sufficient, or do you feel you need more?
- Are your relationships providing enough intimacy, or do you feel you need more?

Here are questions about *withdrawal symptoms*:

- How do you feel when someone or something threatens to take away your possessions, power, or relationships?
- In the past, when you have suffered loss, have you experienced stress reactions such as anxiety, irritability, and so on?
- Can you comfortably go a week or two (or three?) without your favorite behavior, person, or achievement?

Here are questions about *self-deception*:

- Do you make excuses, offer denials, or play other tricks with yourself to rationalize acquiring more of what you love (possessions, power, intimacy)?
- Have friends or family commented (perhaps trying to drop a hint) that you are more attached to certain behaviors, possessions, or people than you think you are?
- Have you said to yourself on more than one occasion, "I can handle this; it's no big deal"?

Here are questions about *loss of willpower*:

- Have you made resolutions to change areas of your life that you felt were getting out of hand? Were you successful in all those resolutions?

- Are there areas about which you won't make such a resolution because you know you can't meet it?

Here is a question about *distortion of attention*:

- Where and when does your concern for certain behaviors, possessions, opportunities, or even people "kidnap" your attention and eclipse genuine love and availability for God? For others? For yourself?

THE ROAD LESS TRAVELED

The way of the heart is the road less traveled. Jesus said, "But small is the gate and narrow the road that leads to life, and only a few find it" (Matthew 7:14). As you think about the lives of the people around you, what is the obvious implication of this verse? How many people do you know who are taking the way of the heart?

To take the road less traveled, we must first allow desire to be rekindled. In the last chapter, we said, "Jesus invites us to thirst. Satan invites us to control." The reason we must allow our thirst to grow is that all our other lovers really serve to deaden our desire, placate it. For example, Brent said that our true desire is for God, that he is what we are chasing in all those other things. Does that sound true but far-off and spiritual?

WINDOW

When I no more can stir my soul to move,
And life is but the ashes of a fire;
When I can but remember that my heart
Once used to live and love, long and aspire—
Oh, be thou then the first, the one thou art;
Be thou the calling, before all answering love,
And in me wake hope, fear, boundless desire.

GEORGE MACDONALD, *DIARY OF AN OLD SOUL*

The central quality of our other lovers is that they are within reach. Think about yours. Do you have to wait in trust upon God, or can you just go get them?

MacDonald spoke of holding the heart an "empty cup." What will you let go of in order to allow your heart to be empty for a while—"athirst and empty," as MacDonald said, "for God's breath to fill"?[47]

Giving up our other lovers often feels like a personal death. Brent told the story of the man who wept upon breaking off his affair, even though he knew it was the right thing to do. What do you expect will cause you sorrow to let go of?

══ IF YOU ARE FEELING . . . ══

Many people feel silly that repentance brings with it sorrow or grief over what is being lost or let go. But it's quite natural. After all, those things once meant life to you.

Does it help at all in letting go to realize that our other lovers keep us from loving God? That he looks upon them not so much as an angry judge would look at a crime but as someone would feel when he has been betrayed? That we have broken his heart?

══ TO CLARIFY ══

In addition, full love for God means that we must turn to God over and against other things. If our choice of God is to be made with integrity, we must first have felt other attractions and chosen, painfully, not to make them our gods. True love, then, is not only born of freedom; it is also born of a difficult choice. A mature and meaningful love must say something like, "I have experienced other goodnesses, and they are beautiful, but it is You, my true heart's desire, whom I choose above all."

GERALD MAY, *ADDICTION AND GRACE*

The choice May refers to is a vital one and a crucial step toward freedom. But it does not mean that we go on to win the battle against our other lovers through sheer willpower. Not at all. Brent said that the way of the heart (the road less traveled) takes us to the edge of an abyss, the aching abyss of our own heart.

We cannot fill it; we cannot make it go away. All we can do is invite Jesus into that place. John Donne, in the poem "Batter My Heart," wrote that we will never be "chaste" (meaning pure of heart, free from all our other lovers) until God "ravishes" us.[48] Why is that?

Would you like God to ravish you? Can you pray Donne's poem as your own heart prayer?

WINDOWS

Film
The Accidental Tourist (Warner, 1988).

Music
"The Needle and the Damage Done" by Neil Young, from *Unplugged* (Reprise Records, 1993).

Book
Addiction and Grace by Gerald May (New York: HarperCollins, 1988). This is truly a remarkable little book. I read it—and recommend it to many—for spiritual growth.

1 0

ON THE ROAD

But we who would be born again indeed, must wake our souls
unnumbered times a day.

GEORGE MACDONALD[49]

YOUR INITIAL REACTION

In two or three minutes, jot down the things that struck you when you read this
chapter. What were your initial thoughts, emotions, impressions?

I felt . . .

I realized . . .

I wanted . . .

━━ PRAYER OF BEGINNING ━━

Blessed are those whose strength is in you,
*   whose hearts are set on pilgrimage.*
As they pass through the Valley of [Weeping],
*   they make it a place of springs. . . .*
They go from strength to strength,
*   till each appears before God in Zion* (Psalm 84:5-7).

Dear Jesus, help me now to set my heart on pilgrimage. Let me be a pilgrim of the heart. Lead me away from all that has held me back. Open my eyes to the Romance all around me. Help me to see your unfolding story in the hours of my days. And grant me, by your strength, to live with faith, hope, and love as I journey forward. I ask this in your name. Amen.

━━ TO CLARIFY ━━

Here are the central truths of this chapter:

- We must set out now on our journey, become pilgrims of the heart.
- The Sacred Romance is played out in our daily lives—if we have the eyes to see.
- As we face the dragons and nits along our way, we are redeemed into our true identity, and we vindicate the heart of God.
- Let us bring along faith, hope, and love—or memory, imagination, and a passion for glory.

EYES FOR THE ROMANCE

Chapter 10 tries to bring all that we've learned into the reality of our daily lives. How do we live this stuff? "'What does all this look like in real life?' How is God wooing us through flat tires, bounced checks, and rained-out picnics? What is he after as we face cancer, sexual struggles, and abandonment? Does knowing that we are his Beloved make any difference at all? Would recognizing Satan's temptations and our less-wild lovers help us to live as freer men and women? What difference does this make anyhow?

"The short answer is, it gives us *a way of seeing that reveals life for the romantic journey it truly is.*"

━━━━━━━━━━━ **IF YOU ARE FEELING . . .** ━━━━━━━━━━━

A way of looking at life? That's it? It may at first seem small potatoes, but think again: "It all depends on how you look at it" is truer than we think. Some people see Jesus of Nazareth as simply a good man, a religious teacher. Others see him as the Son of God, their truest heart's desire. Which ones get to experience his presence and love in their lives? Perspective makes all the difference in the world.

━━━━━━━━━━━━━━━━━━━━━━━━━━━━━━━━━━━━━━━

Think of a time in your life, or an event, that was changed through a change in perspective. What did you see that you hadn't seen before? How did your new outlook or understanding of the situation change the way you responded or felt about it?

In Ephesians 1:18–23, Paul prayed that the eyes of our hearts will be opened to see three things. What are they? How do they relate to all that we've been saying about life in the Sacred Romance? (You might find it helpful to read a translation that is newer to you, such as *The Message* or the New Living Translation.)

I tell the story of a trial I endured at work several years ago, all the pain I went through, and how I never once stopped to consider what God was up to until Brent asked that question. I was a "practical agnostic," meaning that for all practical purposes, I was living as though God wasn't involved in the details. Most of us live that way. Think of something you are currently facing—a difficulty of some kind. What is God up to? Have you stopped to ask the question? Our journey "rests entirely on our ability to see life from the basis of that question."

SETTING OUT

"We are faced with a decision that grows with urgency each passing day: Will we leave our small stories behind and venture forth to follow our Beloved into the Sacred Romance? The choice to become a pilgrim of the heart can happen any day and we can begin our journey from any place." Would you rather be Bilbo Baggins or Robinson Crusoe? The adventurer, caught up in a great journey, or the survivor, hunkered down for survival? Why?

"When he sets out, Bunyan's Pilgrim has no map, no itinerary, no step-by-step travelogue with each day's adventure carefully planned out." What is the central aspect of every adventure; what do they all have in common? It's the element of the *unknown*, of course. The path of the heart, as Brent described back in chapter 9, takes a turn into the thicket and we can't see beyond that where it may lead.

What are you unclear about in your life right now? How do you feel about the lack of clarity, and what are you doing as a result?

LISTEN TO YOUR HEART

Aren't you disappointed—maybe even a little irritated—to realize I'm not going to lay all this out in several easy-to-follow steps?

We need to be very careful about insisting on a plan. It can stop our journey cold in its tracks. The path turns off into the thicket, but don't let that scare you. It's the nature of God's adventures, the way he writes our journey. Have you been told that before? Or have you been led to believe that the Christian life was memorizing principles, applying them to your life, and stepping up each rung of the ladder neatly and cleanly? Which is truer to life?

TO CLARIFY

Naturally, we are inclined to be so mathematical and calculating that we look upon uncertainty as a bad thing. . . . Certainty is the mark of the common-sense life: gracious uncertainty is the mark of the spiritual life. To be certain of God means we are uncertain in all our ways, we do not know what a day may bring forth. This is generally said with a sigh of sadness, it should be rather an expression of breathless expectation.

OSWALD CHAMBERS, *MY UTMOST FOR HIS HIGHEST*[50]

"So much of the journey now involves a letting go of all that once brought us life. We turn away from . . . the false selves we have lived out, the strengths we have used to make a place for ourselves and all our false loves, and we venture forth in our hearts to trace the steps of the One who said, 'Follow me.' In a way, it means that we stop *pretending*: that life is better than it is, that we are happier than we are, that the false selves we present to the world are really us." What do you need to stop pretending about and be more honest? Is life everything you want it to be? Are you totally and completely fulfilled in your small story? Is the person you present to the world the real you?

WINDOW

Let's return to "Along the Road," the song I recommended in chapter 1:

Along the road
your path may wander
A pilgrim's faith may fail
Absence makes the heart grow fonder
Darkness obscures the trail
Cursing the quest
Courting disaster
Measureless nights forebode
Moments of rest
Glimpses of laughter
Are treasured along the road

Along the road
Your steps may stumble
Your thoughts may start to stray
But through it all a heart held humble
Levels and lights your way

What must you leave behind now, as Pilgrim did? What "abiding places" of the heart? Is there something in the physical realm you need to leave behind as well?

One of the most important things we need new eyes to see is this: The things that have captured our hearts have done so because the Romance was calling to us through them. As Lewis said, "It was not in them, it only came *through* them. . . . They are not the thing itself; they are only the scent of a flower we have not found."[51] Can you see what is calling to you through your old lovers?

DRAGONS AND NITS

What struck you about Mary's story in this chapter, the woman who struggled with her teeth? Have you faced something similar? What deep questions did it raise for you?

What words did the adversary jump in with? What was his spin on things?

Was anyone there to help you interpret it in light of the Romance? If there had been, what difference might it have made?

"If we'll take time to reflect, the nits of our lives and the way we typically respond to them both have a *theme*, a pattern that reveals something important about our heart, something God is after." Take that time to reflect right now. Using your journal, take ten minutes and write down several trials you are facing or have recently faced. They can be small or large or both. Now, how did each one make you feel? What was your heart tempted to believe in each situation? How did you respond? What heart place did you resort to in order to deal with it or to find comfort? Is there a theme?

"Both dragons and nits take us into the deep places of the soul, uncovering the sentences we have long lived by." What are those sentences for you? What have the trials revealed?

WINDOW

The Boys in the Boat, set in 1936, follows the remarkable exploits of the junior varsity rowing team at the University of Washington. In one pivotal scene, Al Ulbrickson, the coach, decides to risk his job by sending the JV team ahead of the more experienced varsity team to compete against other college teams for a berth in the Olympics. Al recognizes what no one else sees: it is the JV team that has the true potential to win. Al's faith in the JV team proves to be well placed, as they upset Navy, Cal, and the other privileged Eastern schools to earn a spot in the Olympics. A great story about not only facing the "dragons and nits" in our lives but also about stepping into the destiny God has for us when we are called.

This is one of the hardest lessons to learn: God will actually wound us in the place of our deepest wounds so that he may heal us. The reason is because we stay far away from those wounds and those deep questions until we are *taken* there. "I prayed that God would simply take away the trials in our marriage, but he didn't." What is God taking you into these days? What have you been asking God to take away or change that he hasn't?

What is he up to? Have you asked him? *"For only when we are present in the deep sentences can God speak to them."*

THE WAGER

Act III of the Sacred Romance put the heart of God on trial. As we saw in the opening chapters of Job, Satan questioned God's heart and used his people to try to accuse him. He said to God, "When the going gets tough, no one will really trust you; no one will really love you; no one will choose you."

We are now central players in that drama, witnesses on the stand for God. "When we face a decision to fall back or press on, the whole universe holds its breath—angels, demons, our friends and foes, and the Trinity itself—watching with bated breath to see what we will do." What difference does it make to you to know that you play before an audience, that all heaven holds its breath, that your simple choices vindicate the heart of God?

WINDOW

In "Show the Way" (a song I quoted in chapter 5), David Wilcox sings about this moment in Act III:

> So now the stage is set.
> Feel your own heart beating in your chest.
> This life's not over yet.
> So we get up on our feet and do our best.
> We play against the fear.
> We play against the reasons not to try.
> We're playing for the tears burning in the happy angel's eyes.

Think about the things you are currently facing. What choices can you make right now that will silence the adversary's accusations that no one will really side with God?

Something else happens when we live in the Sacred Romance. "As we grow into the love of God and the freedom of our own hearts, we grow in our ability to cast our vote on behalf of God. Our acts of love and sacrifice, the little decisions to leave our false loves behind and the great struggles of our heart reveal to the world our true identity: We really are the sons and daughters of God." How have you been "revealed" this year? How have your choices revealed that you are a son or daughter of God?

WINDOW

There is a remarkable scene of this sort of "revealing" in a marvelous film called *Hoosiers*, based on a true story about a small-town high school basketball team that goes on to win the state championship in the 1950s. When the coach, played by Gene Hackman, invites the town drunk, "Shooter" (Dennis Hopper), to be his assistant coach, everyone is shocked. But Hackman sees something no one else sees: He sees Shooter's glory. He knows there is more to him than the small story he has been living. At a crucial moment, Hackman gets himself kicked out of a game so that Shooter will be forced to step up and be the man he really is. With all eyes on him, Shooter calls the winning play, and his redemption is sealed.

WHAT TO BRING ALONG

"Our journey begins with desire, 'not for a raise,' says the poet David Whyte, 'but for another life.' Desire sets us on our way, yet what will keep desire alive? Enemies of desire lurk all along the way." What are some of the enemies I mentioned that you recognize from your own journey?

"One of the most poisonous of all Satan's whispers is simply, 'Things will never change.' That lie kills expectation, trapping our heart forever in the present." Have you heard that lie recently? In what area of your life? Or where have you no expectation that things will improve?

"Desire," I said, "is kept alive by imagination, the antidote to resignation." Have you ever thought of it that way—that you can't outdream God? Why do you suppose God gave us imagination in the first place?

And what are you allowing yourself to dream about these days?

"Life on the road [also] requires recollection of our Love's past deeds on our behalf." Faith is built on remembering what God has done.

TO CLARIFY

When the young shepherd David volunteered to face Goliath, King Saul tried to discourage him:

> "You are not able to go out against this Philistine and fight him; you are only a young man, and he has been a warrior from his youth." But David said to Saul, "Your servant has been keeping his father's sheep. When a lion or a bear came and carried off a sheep from the flock, I went after it, struck it and rescued the sheep from its mouth. When it turned on me, I seized it by its hair, struck it and killed it. . . . The LORD who rescued me from the paw of the lion and the paw of the bear will rescue me from the hand of this Philistine" (1 Samuel 17:33–35, 37).

David remembered God's faithfulness from times past, and it gave him courage and strength to face the giant.

Take a few moments now to recall (and write down in your journal) the ways in which God has shown up for you in the past. What are the lions and bears from which God has delivered you? (It is vital that you write these things down. If you haven't begun to already, make a regular habit of capturing God's answers to prayer in your journal so that you can revisit them from time to time to gain new strength.)

"The road we travel will take us into the battle to restore beauty in all things, chief among them the hearts of those we know. We grow in glory so that we might assist others in doing so; we give our glory to increase theirs. In order to fulfill the purpose of our journey, we will need a passion to increase glory; we will need *love*." Whose hearts are you in the battle for these days? Write their names here. What is in the way of their glory? How might your own heart offer what they need or at least draw them toward it?

TO CLARIFY

The three essentials I list are taken from 1 Corinthians 13:13: "And now these three remain: faith, hope and love." These are not merely virtues or nice habits to have. They are *forces*, the power centers of the Christian life. But because most of us have heard of them so many times, and thought of them largely in moral or spiritual terms, I describe them as imagination, remembering, and a passion to increase glory—which, of course, they are.

WINDOWS

Film

The Boys in the Boat (Amazon MGM Studios, 2023).

Hoosiers (MGM/UA, 1986).

Music

"Along the Road," title track from *Along the Road* by Susan Ashton, Margaret Becker, and Christine Dente (Sparrow Records, 1994).

"Show the Way" by David Wilcox, from *Big Horizon* (A&M Records, 1994).

Books

Pilgrim's Progress by John Bunyan (many editions available). Now that you've seen things through the lens of the Sacred Romance, this classic from the late 1600s will come alive for you. A great allegory of our journey.

11

DESERT COMMUNION: LEARNING TO LIVE ON HEAVEN'S SHORES

Our nature makes us wish for rest, that is to say, an increase in being.

SAINT AUGUSTINE[52]

YOUR INITIAL REACTION

In two or three minutes, jot down the things that struck you when you read this chapter. What were your initial thoughts, emotions, impressions?

I felt . . .

I realized . . .

I wanted . . .

PRAYER OF BEGINNING

You, God, are my God,
*   earnestly I seek you;*
I thirst for you,
*   my whole being longs for you,*
in a dry and parched land
*   where there is no water* (Psalm 63:1).

Dear Jesus, allure me; draw me into the desert. Speak tenderly to me there. Block my path so that I cannot but follow you; even though I chase my other lovers, let me not catch them. Alone with you, let me find your love and your salvation. In your name I pray. Amen.

TO CLARIFY

Here are the central truths of this chapter:

- Every courtship, at least every healthy one, is moving toward a deeper heart intimacy.
- We don't go from being strangers to lovers in an instant.
- We must learn to make our home in God.
- There is a place on each of our spiritual journeys where the Spirit desires, therefore, to lead us into the desert.

DEEPER INTIMACY

Back in chapter 1, at the beginning of this journey, we wrote, "What we want to say in these pages is simply this: *Our hearts are telling us the truth—there really is something missing!*" How did you respond to that statement then? How do you respond to it now?

"Every courtship, at least every healthy one, is moving toward a deeper heart intimacy that is the ground for the consummation of the relationship spiritually, emotionally, and physically." How is God courting you these days? Do you see yourself moving toward a deeper heart intimacy? Why—or why not?

TO CLARIFY

In the book of Hosea, we get a stunning picture of God's passionate and jealous pursuit of us—in spite of our whoring after other lovers:

> *"Therefore I will block her path with thornbushes;*
> *I will wall her in so that she cannot find her way.*
> *She will chase after her lovers but not catch them;*
> *she will look for them but not find them.*
> *Then she will say,*
> *'I will go back to my husband as at first,*
> *for then I was better off than now.' . . .*
> *Therefore I am now going to allure her;*
> *I will lead her into the wilderness*
> *and speak tenderly to her. . . .*
>
> *"In that day," declares the LORD,*
> *"you will call me 'my husband';*
> *you will no longer call me 'my master.' . . .*
> *I will betroth you to me forever;*
> *I will betroth you in righteousness and justice,*
> *in love and compassion"* (Hosea 2:6–7, 14, 16, 19).

When you think about the idea of knowing God better, what comes to mind? As Brent said, "Images of learning more about him immediately come to mind. With a sigh, we consider what book we might buy or what Bible study we might attend to understand more clearly God's attributes." But is that the way you want to get to really know your most intimate love? Does it draw you in the way in which Adam "knew Eve his wife" (Genesis 4:1 KJV) and she gave birth as a result? Which way of knowing are you pursuing?

Look at the two conversations in this chapter between lovers in the sidewalk café. Which captures your Christian life up till now? Which would you like to capture in the next chapter of your relationship with God?

IF YOU ARE FEELING . . .

I do want a deeper intimacy with God. But even now, I'm somewhat fearful, and I don't know how to get there. It's helpful at this point to remember these words that Brent wrote: "We don't go from being strangers to intimate allies in an instant." It takes time; there is a natural development of any relationship. So the question then becomes, "How is God drawing me, and how am I responding?"

Thinking more about a relationship that is deepening, we must know where to go to hear God's voice. Where does God whisper to us? "God is not 'out there somewhere' in some dramatic way, waiting to commune with us by earthquake or fire or signs in the sky. Instead, he desires to talk with us in the quietness of our own heart through his Spirit, who is in us." Is that a new thought to you—that God is whispering within your heart? How do you respond?

TO CLARIFY

Madame Guyon, a true lover of God from the seventeenth century, shares with us the only way to deeper intimacy: "After your conversion. . . . Your spirit instructs your soul that, since God is more present deep within you, He *cannot* be found anywhere else. Henceforth, He *must* be sought within."[53]

That is precisely what Paul taught: "For his Spirit joins with our spirit to affirm that we are God's children" (Romans 8:16 NLT). To hear God's voice within, we must trust our relationship with him; trust that we are now indwelt by his Spirit.

"What do you hear when you listen for that gentle, quiet voice?" Like Brent, do you hear, or feel, a restlessness, a distractedness, bits and pieces of your smaller story, what other people think of you, anger, ego, lust, or simply blankness of spirit?

───── **LISTEN TO** ─────
YOUR HEART

Take a few moments now
to listen for God's voice
within. What happens?

OUR SEARCH FOR AN IDENTITY

The problem is that we are not used to finding our deep identity in God, and so we try to find our identity in activity. Celebrities and pro athletes are classic examples. Men often try to "anchor" themselves to some sort of competence or performance. Can you see that? If you are a man, what is yours? Where do you go for a sense of self? (If you are a woman, think about the men in your life.)

Women, for the most part, try to ground themselves in being valued for their external beauty (or, having failed, they go to the opposite and try to hide their femininity, which is just the reverse side of the same issue). If you are a woman, can you see this in your life? Where do you go for a sense of self? (If you are a man, think about the women in your life.)

Reflect on the movies and television shows you've seen recently. What is the underlying message of this question: *What makes a man a man and a woman a woman?* Give a few examples from what you've seen.

"As Christians, we often feel the ungrounded restlessness of our ontological lightness even in our prayers." Listen to yourself pray. What are your prayers like? Are they mostly checking in, apologizing, or taking care of business, getting things covered? Do they sound businesslike, or intimate and loving?

Jesus said his yoke was easy and his burden light (see Matthew 11:30). Is that how it feels to you? Has it occurred to you that if Christianity does not feel easy and light, you may have bought into a version different from the one Jesus offers?

Brent asked himself a question we all need to ask: *"If I'm not abiding in Jesus, then where is it that I abide?"* He noticed that when he was feeling anxious or tired, or irritable or vulnerable, there were certain sentences he would say to himself, certain emotions he would go to for comfort. "I had always thought of these things as just bad habits. I began to see that they were much more; they were spiritual abiding places that were my comforters and friends in a very spiritual way." When you are feeling those same things, where do you go?

Here is what the whole issue comes down to: We must learn to make our home in God. "I have made my home in you," said Jesus. "You must learn to make your home in me" (from John 15). It is coming to see that our spiritual life is not about *doing* but about *being*. Is that what you've been raised to believe? Is it what your church practices (look at what the people in leadership do, who they hold up as models of maturity)?

Brent said he "began to reject the cynical thoughts when they came to comfort me and replace them with words of faith. . . . Rather than indulge in my less-wild lovers, I began at times to tighten on the team the rigid rein and simply stand (rest) in faith." What are the new sentences, from Jesus to you, that you must grasp to reject the old abiding places?

Notice how this plays out in such simple—and therefore *unnoticed*—ways. Our abiding places are so *familiar*. That is why MacDonald said, "We who would be born again indeed, must wake our souls unnumbered times a day." We must deepen our self-awareness as we go through the ins and outs of our regular days

We must be listening to our heart through the day. Would you describe yourself as a self-aware person? If not, why not?

A WARNING

I used to be prepared for the enemy's attacks in more obvious settings, such as during times of "ministry." But I have come to see again and again that attacks most often come whenever growth and freedom occur in our hearts. Brent said that spiritual warfare began to intensify as the adversary saw him breaking agreement with the old lies and thus rejecting the enemy's strongholds in his heart. This will happen to you as well. Remember, you are at war, and the battle is for your heart.

SO WHERE DO WE GO FOR A SENSE OF SELF?

"We all want to be someone's hero or someone's beauty, to be in a relationship of heroic proportions. We need to feel free to admit this without embarrassment. It is a core longing God himself placed within us and a deep part of our identity as men and women." Do you feel how deep that longing runs in you? And do you feel free to admit it without embarrassment?

The problem is not the longing. "It is in how we go about being heroes and beauties that is the issue. . . . God calls Israel to repent by admitting her weariness and fainting. Instead, she looks for ways to use her personal assets to redeem herself." Two questions for you: How does it feel to think that God is inviting you to "faint" into his arms? And what are the ways you are trying to redeem yourself instead?

Was it surprising to consider that "the problem is not that people are not important enough to us. It is that they are *too* important—we need their approval too much"? Think about how you are living. What are the expectations of others that are currently shaping the way you act and how you spend your time?

To be honest, most of our contemporary churches operate on this system of guilt, the idea that if you are not *doing* a lot, you're not a good Christian. What can you stop doing for the sake of your own soul? What activities can you drop?

IF YOU ARE FEELING . . .

Drop that? But I can't! If you immediately feel guilty about stopping a certain activity, then what is the motivation that keeps you in that activity? Is it not guilt? Is that the way Jesus speaks to us? Now you *know* what to drop!

THE DESERT TRADITION

"There is a place on each of our spiritual journeys where the Spirit also desires to lead us into the desert. We hear him calling to us in the restlessness and weariness of our own heart." Some years ago, a friend of mine was led by God to leave her life in Colorado and spend seven weeks on the coast of Spain, simply for rest and restoration. She wasn't ill; she was just like the rest of us, in desperate need of rest. Think for a moment—wouldn't you love to cut out all the busyness of your life, all the duty and demand and flurry of activity, and simply *rest*? Where would you go?

TO CLARIFY

I think most of us read the temptation story of Jesus in the wilderness and think, *How unfair. Satan hits him at his weakest moment, when there was no one and nothing around for Jesus to lean on.* But we are quite mistaken. Dallas Willard points out in *The Spirit of the Disciplines*:

> Today, sustained withdrawal from society into solitude seems to indicate weakness, suffering, flight, or failure rather than great strength, joy and effectiveness. Believing that, we, for instance, thoroughly misunderstand the context of Jesus' temptations after his baptism (Matthew 4). The Spirit, we are told, led him into the wilderness to be tempted by the devil. Was this not to put Jesus in the weakest

possible position before Satan, starving and alone in the wilds? Most to whom I have spoken about this matter are shocked at the suggestion that the "wilderness," the place of solitude and deprivation, was actually *the place of strength and strengthening* for our Lord and that the Spirit led him there—as he would lead *us* there—to ensure that Christ was in the best possible condition for the trial.[54]

"In order to learn who we are, we must have a place in our lives where we are removed from the materialism, entertainment, diversion, and busyness that the Vanity Fair of our society and culture immerse us in." Where can this place be for you? What will you do to begin a regular practice of silence and solitude for the sake of your soul?

TO CLARIFY

How do we go about "doing rest"? Here are a few suggestions:

- Turn off all distractions in the car—the cell phone, radio, and everything else. Let all your travel time be silent time.
- Turn off the media in your home. The news is just not that important; neither are your favorite movies or shows. Far, far more important is protecting the life of your heart.
- Set aside lunch as a sacred time. Don't fill it with business, shopping, meetings, or what have you. Find a quiet spot and spend it there.
- Set your alarm to get up earlier; even fifteen minutes can make a huge difference. Don't fill the time with Christian activities; use it for silence and solitude.
- If you are awakened in the middle of the night, don't fight it. Accept the invitation to communion.

I want you to take an hour and give this a go. Find a place where you will not be disturbed. It may be in the mountains or a secluded spot. Sometimes I have to hide in the bathroom so as not to be found. Take your journal with you. And let these guidelines shepherd you through your experience:

1. What will we find when we get to our wilderness, our desert, our place of rest? "The first thing we encounter is not rest, but fear, and a compulsion to return to activity. . . . Our emptiness is often the first thing we find when we face honestly the story going on in our heart. It is the desert's gift to us." Don't be afraid or feel like a spiritual failure; just stay with it. Be honest, write it down, and continue.

2. "Resting in Jesus is not applying a spiritual formula to ourselves as a kind of fix-it. It is the essence of repentance. It is letting our heart tell us where we are in our own story so that Jesus can minister to us out of the Story of his love for us." We need to allow time and space for our heart to speak. What is your heart saying next?

3. Once we begin to connect with our deep heart, we often encounter grief or sorrow. Let it come, and let the tears flow.

4. Other times, we encounter a deep-seated accusation or sentence that has long ruled us. In response, we need to stay with a simple truth, hold it in our hearts, as Brent did with the sentence, "Jesus, you are faithful to cleanse me from all my sins."

5. You may encounter spiritual warfare, as Jesus did in his wilderness. Answer as he did, with Scripture, with rebuke (out loud—for the evil one cannot read your mind).

6. Then, we give to Jesus whatever our hearts have spoken to us about; we invite him *into* those places of our heart, let him minister to us. We listen for his voice deep in our heart, let him speak to us about all we are experiencing. (Write this down too. You'll probably forget it by the next day.)

WINDOW

I lift my eyes when I am troubled
I lift my hands
I lift my heart
And there I stand, knowing nothing can defeat me
Just as long as I know where you are
In you alone
Is where I find my comfort
In you alone
You're my only hope
In you alone
My heart has found a resting place

KIM HILL, "YOU ALONE"

WINDOW

There is a beautiful picture of healing and transformation in the film I mentioned in chapter 1, *Enchanted April*. The effect on the characters of a month away, set apart from their less-wild lovers, is simply amazing . . . and deeply true to what God has taught us. The sour wife becomes passionate again toward her husband; he, in turn, gives up his other lovers for her. The solitary and resigned spinster lets others into her life, warming to relationship again. The hectic businessman becomes a kind and gentle soul; the glamour queen discovers her true beauty through the "eyes" of a man going blind. You must watch this story.

WINDOWS

Film
Enchanted April (Miramax Films, 1992).

Music

Out of Africa motion picture soundtrack (MCA Records, 1985).

"You Alone" by Kim Hill, from *Arms of Mercy* (Star Song Records, 1998).

Books

The Way of the Heart by Henri Nouwen (New York: Seabury Press, 1981).

The Spirit of the Disciplines by Dallas Willard (San Francisco: HarperSanFrancisco, 1988).

COMING HOME

The door on which we have been knocking all our lives will open at last.

C. S. LEWIS[55]

YOUR INITIAL REACTION

In two or three minutes, jot down the things that struck you when you read this chapter. What were your initial thoughts, emotions, impressions?

I felt . . .

I realized . . .

I wanted . . .

PRAYER OF BEGINNING

You make known to me the path of life;
you will fill me with joy in your presence,
with eternal pleasures at your right hand (Psalm 16:11).

Dear Jesus, fill my heart with hope by releasing my imagination for the life to come. Let me live in anticipation. Lift my eyes beyond the immediate, the tyranny of the here and now, and let me see the wonders of the kingdom that is just around the corner. Help me to embrace this so deeply that it cannot be taken away from me. In your name I pray. Amen.

TO CLARIFY

Here are the central truths of this chapter:

- Our hearts cannot live without hope.
- But most of us think this life is as good as it gets.
- That's because we've lost our imagination for the life to come.
- But when we look at the longings of our heart, and the promises of Scripture, it truly can take our breath away and restore our hope.

LIVING WITH HOPE

Chapter 12 is about the ending of our story—the ending God has told us to read ahead of time, and for good reason. "Our hearts cannot live without hope." Would you describe yourself as an essentially hopeful person? What would you say you are hoping for?

I tell the story of hope restored on a fly-fishing trip to the Tetons. Can you recall a time when hope was restored to you? What happened? What did it do for your heart?

"If for all practical purposes we believe that this life is our best shot at happiness, if this is as good as it gets, we will live as desperate, demanding, and eventually despairing men and women. We will place on this world a burden it was never intended to bear. We will try to find a way to sneak back into Eden, and when that fails, as it always does, our heart fails as well." Be honest now. Where are most of your hopes for happiness set?

LISTEN TO YOUR HEART

What happens inside you when people start to talk about heaven? Do your ears perk up or does your heart check out?

So, what are your images of heaven? Before reading this chapter, what did you believe would come next?

Do you even think about it much? In an average week or month or year, how often would you say you linger over the hope of heaven and eternity and all that?

A. J. Conyers said, "We live in a world no longer under heaven."[56] How many books have you read on heaven in your life? What percentage is that of all the books you have read? How many sermons on heaven have you heard, say, in a year of fifty-two Sundays?

Where does that leave you in the here and now? Desperate? (Do you feel the urgent need to make something of life now?) Demanding? (Do you get angry when life doesn't go the way you want? Do you spend large amounts of energy arranging a better life for yourself?) Despairing? (Have you given up wanting much at all anymore, not feeling much, just getting by?)

How do you try to "sneak back into Eden"?

When we stop pretending, we realize that "the best human life is unspeakably sad." But instead of turning our hearts toward the life to come, "we feel guilty about our disappointment, as though we ought to be more grateful." Have you felt guilty about your disappointment with life? Do you even let it surface much? Do you feel bad about wanting more?

RECOVERING THE END OF THE STORY

Peter Kreeft writes that a failure of *imagination* is killing us: "Our pictures of Heaven simply do not move us; they are not moving pictures."[57] Think for a moment about the stories and movies you love. What are some of your favorite happy endings? (I always cry at the end of *It's a Wonderful Life*, with George and Mary and the children gathered around the Christmas tree, their friends and family pouring in from all over, emptying their piggy banks just to save their friend, everyone singing "Auld Lang Syne.") Describe a few of yours.

"If our pictures of heaven are to move us, they must be moving pictures. So go ahead—dream a little. Use your imagination; let your heart speak! You were made for Eden, and 'heaven' is Eden's return. Picture the best possible ending to your story you can." Take a few minutes right now to open your journal and write out the things you would *love* to see happen in Act IV. Whom do you long to see there? What do you long to do? Write the best "happy ending" you can think of for your life story.

TO CLARIFY

I did this exercise some years ago when I was flying home from a trip. I was surprised by what came out of my heart's unspoken dreams. Here are a few:

I would *love* to . . .

- be released to be my truest self of all;
- see my father as a young man, strong and loving, and share some great adventure with him;
- see my mother as a young, beautiful woman, tender, vulnerable, and hear her laugh;
- walk with God in Eden in the cool of the day, and be his true friend;
- attend a great banquet with those who love me—eat and drink, dance and laugh, stroll the gardens and be in love;
- fly through the Grand Canyon;
- mountain climb in Patagonia;
- explore coral reefs and tropical lagoons.

Ecclesiastes 3:11 proclaims, "He has also set eternity in the human heart." Have you ever stopped to wonder *where*? Where in our hearts has God set eternity? In our *longings*. "As we have said from chapter 1, there is in the heart of every man, woman, and child an inconsolable longing for intimacy, for beauty, and for adventure." Stop for a moment to let this sink in: Your deepest desires are telling you about what is to come, what you are truly made for. What goes on inside when you consider that?

But isn't heaven sort of a big church service in the sky? I mean, don't we worship God forever and ever? Yes, that's the picture many of us were given. And no wonder we don't hope for heaven. But it's not the picture given to us in Scripture. It's one of many, many images. Perhaps the reason we aren't captivated by it is that our church services are, for the most part, incredibly boring.

But the promise of the life to come goes way, way beyond singing hymns. Thank God.

INTIMACY

"Our longing for intimacy gives us the greatest scent of the joys that lie ahead. Eden was a world of wild intimacy, 'naked and unashamed' (Genesis 2:25). Being left out is one of life's most painful experiences." I tell the story of recess in elementary school and lunch during junior high. What have been your experiences of being left out? How did they make you feel? Were you made to be left out?

Contrast those experiences with others, times in which you were not left out. Have you ever had a surprise party, received an unexpected card in the mail, or been welcomed into a new situation with a warm handshake? Describe a few of those experiences. If only for a moment, did you have "a sense of relief, a taste of being on the inside"?

Have you ever enjoyed yourself at a dinner party, a banquet, a feast of some kind? Picture yourself now walking into "the crowded excitement of the wedding feast of the Lamb, with the sound of a thousand conversations, laughter and music, the clinking of glasses," of being "welcomed to the table by our Lover himself." What do you look forward to? With whom would you love to sit at your table? What would you love to talk about? With whom would you long to have a dance?

"It's not just any kind of party; it is a *wedding* feast. What sets this special feast apart from all others is the unique intimacy of the wedding night." Have you ever considered that *sex* is the picture our God chooses to describe the intimacy that is coming to us? How does it compare to, say, those pictures of heaven as the eternal church service in the sky?

Intimate lovers, family members, and close friends often have special names for each other. Did you have any growing up? What were they? Do you have any now? Think now about the white stone from Revelation 2:17. Knowing it is your "soul's symbol," the name of the one you have truly become, what would you love to see written on your white stone?

"The intimacy that begins between God and his people will be enriched and echoed by our communion with each other." After the Resurrection, the disciples saw and recognized Jesus; they carried on quite normal conversations with him. So we see that when we get to heaven, we will recognize each other. Whom are you longing to see? What conversations do you long to have?

Just stop a moment and let this quote from Lewis sink in: "The door on which we have been knocking all our lives will open at last."[58]

WINDOW

The Impossible follows the story of Doctor Maria Bennett, her husband, Harry, and their three sons. In 2004, the family goes on vacation to Khao Lak, Thailand, when a massive Indian Ocean tsunami hits the area. The family is split up in the midst of the ensuing chaos, and the rest of the movie tracks their journey in being reunited. It's a thrilling story with a great ending that tells us what "returning home" is all about.

BEAUTY

Brent described coming upon the Grand Canyon unexpectedly. I describe experiencing the evening of haunting beauty at the Ritz Carlton in Laguna Beach, flying over the glaciers in Alaska, and my friend's visit to Westminster. What have been some of your most treasured moments of beauty? What happened? Describe the scene. How did it make you feel? What was your experience?

Do you see now that beauty is, in fact, one of the deepest longings of your heart? Do you hear in those moments the echo of eternity?

And what about the brokenness around you—the ugliness of the fallen world? What about its brokenness has brought you grief? Can you hear in your response your longing for things to be restored, for all of life to be beautiful?

Jonathan Edwards wrote that our senses are a vital part of our enjoyment of eternity, that "every faculty will be an inlet of delight." Keeping in mind that God restores the earth as well (see Romans 8:21; Revelation 21:1), what do you long to see and partake of in eternity?

What do you suppose the fruit of the tree of life tastes like? (Think of your most favorite fruit at its ripest, and then write a description.)

And the river of life—what do you imagine it will be like? What is the best drink of water you've ever had?

Jesus said he would not feast or drink wine again until he drinks it with us in the kingdom of heaven (see Luke 22:16–18). Think of a truly great meal you've had, one of your best dining experiences. What would you love to feast on in the kingdom? What would you love to drink? Write a menu for the wedding feast of the Lamb.

ADVENTURE

"What will we do in the New Earth?" How have you answered that question in the past? Does it take your breath away?

Just dream a little: What would you *like* to do if you had all the time in the world spread out before you?

What part of God's great universe would you love to explore? And with whom?

━━━━━━━━━━━━━━━ **TO CLARIFY** ━━━━━━━━━━━━━━━

George MacDonald wrote this to his daughter, who would soon die of tuberculosis:

> I do live expecting great things in the life that is ripening for me and all mine—when we shall have all the universe for our own, and be good merry helpful children in the great house of our Father. Then, darling, you and all will have the grand liberty wherewith Christ makes free—opening his hand to send us out like white doves to range the universe.

THE HEART OF GEORGE MACDONALD[59]

"The parable of the minas in Luke 19 and the talents in Matthew 25 foreshadow a day when we shall exercise our real place in God's economy, the role we have been preparing for in this life. He who has been faithful in the small things will be given even greater adventures, opportunities, responsibilities that are a joy, because it is what we are made for." So, what part of God's creation would you love to be put in charge of? What would you love to develop, care for, watch over?

Think about your very favorite activities—your hobbies, the work you truly love. How are you being prepared in those very things for the role God has for you later? What is it about the things that you love, and do well, that would be sheer joy to do even better in heaven?

ARRIVAL

What was your reaction to the story I told of our treacherous drive through snowy mountain roads, only to find ourselves in the magic of the Wawona Hotel in winter, with lights and garlands and fire and all?

What have been your tastes of "coming home," of arrival, of safe passage to a beautiful and comforting haven?

WINDOW

One of my all-time favorite endings to a movie is in *Apollo 13*, based on the true story of the mission to the moon that runs afoul, and the fight against all odds to bring those men home safely. After everything has been said and done, all the world can do is watch and wait. Will the heat shield hold? Will the parachutes unfold in time? Will the capsule survive the intense heat of reentry? Seconds seem like hours as the astronauts disappear into blackout. All eyes are fixed on the blank television screen. Suddenly the capsule appears, parachutes opening beautifully.

> "Hello, Houston . . . this is *Odyssey*. It's good to see you again."
> *(Cheers. Hugging. Tears.)*
> "*Odyssey*, Houston. Welcome home . . . we're glad to see you."

I've seen it probably twenty times, and I cry even still. It's such a beautiful picture of our journey through danger and the "fiery ordeal," and our homecoming to family and friends.

"And then real life begins." Is there any desire that you can conceive of that will not be met in the life to come? Yes, we might get lost in arguing about the specifics and how it will all happen, but consider this: Is it possible that we can conceive of a better ending to the story than the Master Storyteller himself, the one who created fairy tales?

WINDOWS

Film

The Impossible (Warner Brothers, 2012).

Apollo 13 (Universal, 1995).

Music

The Mission motion picture soundtrack (Virgin Records, 1986). Especially tracks 1, 2, and 11.

Books

The Last Battle by C. S. Lewis (New York: HarperCollins, 2008). The final book in the Chronicles of Narnia; you must read it.

The Weight of Glory by C. S. Lewis (London: Geoffrey Bles Publishers, 1949). His famous sermon on heaven, given during World War II.

The Journey of Desire by John Eldredge (Nashville, TN: Nelson Books, 2016). Especially chapters 7, 8, and 9, devoted to our life to come.

REMEMBERING TOWARD EDEN'S RETURN

The Road goes ever on and on, down from the door where it began. Now far ahead the Road has gone, and I must follow, if I can, pursuing it with eager feet, until it joins some larger way.

J. R. R. TOLKIEN[60]

YOUR INITIAL REACTION

In two or three minutes, jot down the things that struck you when you read this chapter. What were your initial thoughts, emotions, impressions?

I felt . . .

I realized . . .

I wanted . . .

PRAYER OF BEGINNING

Yet I am always with you;
you hold me by my right hand.
You guide me with your counsel,
and afterward you will take me into glory.
Whom have I in heaven but you?
And earth has nothing I desire besides you.
My flesh and my heart may fail,
but God is the strength of my heart
and my portion forever (Psalm 73:23-26).

Dear Jesus, thank you for all you have done for me in this journey. I cannot help praying that you would lead me from this place, on the road I now must travel. Grant me the grace to remember; help me not to forget. When I stray, come and find me. When I want to quit, give me courage to press on. Above all, rouse in me desire, that I may ever thirst and seek after the true life. In your name I pray. Amen.

TO CLARIFY

Here are the central truths of this chapter:

- The road goes on now before us, and all we can do is follow it as best we can.
- When the going gets rough, we're going nowhere without desire—so let desire grow!
- Of all our enemies on the road, the greatest is forgetfulness—so prepare to remember!
- The Sacred Romance calls to us every moment of our lives—just keep an open heart and watch for it, listen for it.

DRAWING TO A CLOSE

We began a journey many, many hours, days, even months ago. "We set out to discover if there is in the wide world out there a reality that corresponds to the world within our heart. Hopefully, we have helped you see in new ways that Chesterton was right: Romance is the deepest thing in life; it is deeper even than reality." And now that our journey together is drawing to a close, I'm curious—have we? Have we helped you discover the Romance? Are you more aware? In what ways?

At the end of the exercises in chapter 1, I said, "It is possible to recover the lost life of our heart and with it the intimacy, beauty, and adventure of life with God. To do so, we must leave what is familiar and comfortable . . . and take a journey." I asked you at that time what you were hoping to find. Take a look at your answer. What were your expectations at the beginning of this journey? Have they been met? What has God done for you in these pages?

LIVING FROM DESIRE

The road goes on now before us, and all we can do is follow it as best we can. But remember: "When the going gets rough, we're going nowhere without desire. And the going will get rough." The going will get rough—that's a very important thing to remember as we think about our journey ahead. Where do you expect your difficulties will come from?

── **LISTEN TO** ──
YOUR HEART

Are you aware that
it's not going to be an easy
journey from here? Will
knowing that stop you?

The Bible tells us we have three basic enemies: the world, the devil, and the flesh. "The world, the minions of darkness, and your own double-mindedness are all set against you." What will each of them throw at you in the weeks ahead? In an effort to prepare your heart for the battle and journey, it would be helpful to think that through a bit. Start with the "world"—the people around you, the city and culture in which you live. What will they do to try to keep you from pursuing the Romance and freedom of heart?

══════════════ **TO CLARIFY** ══════════════

So I saw in my dream that the man began to run. Now, he had
not run far from his own door, but his wife and children per-
ceiving it, began to cry after him to return; but the man put his
fingers in his ears, and ran on, crying, Life! Life! Eternal life! So he
looked not behind him, but fled . . . The neighbors also came out
to see him run; and as he ran, some mocked, others threatened,
and some cried after him to return.

JOHN BUNYAN, *THE PILGRIM'S PROGRESS*[61]

When Pilgrim ran from the City of Destruction, all the other players in his small story tried to lure him back. When that didn't work, they tried threatening him back. This will happen to you as well. Be prepared, and do as Pilgrim did—press on, running if you must.

To be more specific, what will the other players in your story do to hurt your progress as a pilgrim of the heart? What will they pull you back to or threaten you with?

And how will the devil try to set you back? What temptations will he use? What distractions? What form of intimidation?

And how about your flesh? What is your own double-mindedness that will betray you in your journey? Who are the old lovers that will call to your heart?

So then, what was the secret of Jesus' life? How did he do it—finish the race so well?

"'The whole life of the good Christian,' said Augustine, 'is a holy longing.' Sadly, many of us have been led to believe that somehow we ought to want less, not more. We have this sense that we should atone for our longings, apologize that we feel such deep desire. Shouldn't we be more content?" At this point in your journey, how are you handling your desire? Are you letting it grow or trying to diminish it, apologizing for it even?

What is contentment? How would you have defined it before reading this chapter? How would your church define it?

"Contentment can only happen as we increase desire, let it run itself out toward its fulfillment.... Our Hero is the example. He's run on before us and he's made it, he's there now. His life assures us it can be done, but only through passionate desire for the joy set before us." What can you expect in the journey of desire? Will your desire be fulfilled?

─────────────── **TO CLARIFY** ───────────────

In fact, we have only three choices in life: to be *alive and haunted* by the Romance, to be *addicted* because we gave our heart away, or to be *dead*, having killed all desire. There are no other options.

"Desire often feels like an enemy." Why? From your own story, past and present, how have you felt desire as an enemy?

So what do we do with disappointment? "Awakened souls are often disappointed, but our disappointment can lead us onward, actually increasing our desire and lifting it toward its true passion." How have you mishandled your disappointment in the past? What false comforters have you turned to? If it doesn't mean something's wrong with you, if disappointment is to be expected, how might you let disappointment work *for* you now?

=== **IF YOU ARE FEELING . . .** ===

Is it all just struggle from here on out? Not at all. I don't mean to paint a grim picture; all I want is for you to be well armed against your enemies. But there is great joy on the road ahead. As Peter said, there is joy in our journey, even though we face trials along the way (see 1 Peter 1:6). Michael Card sings in "Joy in the Journey":

> There is a joy in the journey
> There's a light we can love on the way
> There is a wonder and wildness to life
> And freedom for those who obey . . .
> And all those who seek it will find it

I also love Van Morrison's song "Bright Side of the Road":

> From the dark end of the street
> To the bright side of the road
> We'll be lovers once again
> On the bright side of the road.
> Let's enjoy it while we can
> Won't you help me sing my song
> From the dark end of the street
> To the bright side of the road

REHEARSING THE STORY

"If we choose the way of desire, our greatest enemy on the road ahead is not the Arrows, nor Satan, nor our false lovers. The most crippling thing that besets the pilgrim heart is simply forgetfulness." Why is forgetting such an enemy?

So, what is your plan to remember? I mean, *specifically*, what is *your* plan? You will need one!

TO CLARIFY

We all forget, all the time. Our hearts are like sieves or colanders or leaky faucets. We need help in remembering. Let me suggest one approach: Go over this workbook again. You've spent so much time and effort on it—don't just set it aside. Take a few weeks to read through it, review your answers, think about what you've learned, notice the changes that have taken place from the beginning till now.

In an effort to refresh your memory, take a few minutes now and leaf through the workbook, chapter by chapter, beginning to end. What are the major things that struck you? What were the key revelations from each chapter? Write them down here:

The Lost Life of the Heart

An Unknown Romancing

The Message of the Arrows

A Story Big Enough to Live In

The Wildness of God

God the Ageless Romancer

The Beloved

The Adversary: Legends of the Fall

Less-Wild Lovers

On the Road

Desert Communion: Learning to Live on Heaven's Shores

Coming Home

As I mentioned in the Epilogue, there are truths that speak to our heart and truths that don't. It's not just *what* we remember, but *how* we remember. "Our acts of remembering must therefore involve both essential truths and dramatic narrative.[62] I believe we need to hold the creeds in one hand and our favorite forms of art in the other. There are films, books, poems, songs, and paintings I return to again and again . . . they all tell me about some part of the Sacred Romance."

WINDOW

Let me share one more of my all-time favorite films—Shakespeare's *Henry V*. Brent quoted from it in chapter 5, the St. Crispin's Day speech. It stirs my heart and brings me to tears every time I see it.

The story goes like this: King Henry's loving courage has captured the hearts of his people, and he has led them into battle against the enemy, just as our Captain has done. Late in the war, the mighty army has been reduced to a small band of warriors. They have been marching for days through the rain and mud; many are sick and many more are wounded. They come to the field of Agincourt, where they are met by the entire French army.

They are outnumbered five to one; the French are rested and fresh, and they have a mounted cavalry. The English have none. Faced with such odds (and don't they feel like the odds *you* face?), the men are about to lose heart. But Henry calls them up into a larger story:

> This day is call'd the feast of Crispian:
> He that outlives this day, and comes safe home,
> Will stand a tip-toe when this day is nam'd,
> And rouse him at the name of Crispian.
> He that shall live this day, and see old age,
> Will yearly on the vigil feast his neighbors,
> And say, "Tomorrow is Saint Crispian."
> Then will he strip his sleeve and show his scars,
> And say, "These wounds I had on Crispin's day."
> Old men forget; yet all shall be forgot,
> But he'll remember with advantages
> What feats he did that day; then shall our names,

Familiar in their mouths as household words . . .
Be in their flowing cups freshly remember'd.
This story shall the good man teach his son;
And Crispin Crispian shall ne'er go by,
From this day to the ending of the world,
But we in it shall be remembered.
We few, we happy few, we band of brothers.

ACT IV, SCENE III

The English go on to win the battle—a *true* story (!) and one of many we need to keep at hand in our journey.

What are the things you need to return to for your heart? What are the films, songs, books, poems, and so on? List as many as you can.

Are they at hand? What can you do to keep them nearby?

Also, we need a few companions for the journey. We remember *in community*. This is a very, very difficult journey to take alone. I don't recommend it; and Scripture warns us not to try. Who will be your companions on this journey? Whom can you invite to journey with you?

IF YOU ARE FEELING . . .

But I haven't got anyone. No one I know is walking this path. Then you must pray for God to bring a companion. There will rarely be more than a few, but you need a few.

Our companions are not merely with us in the present. We must draw upon those who have gone before. As I lamented in this chapter, "One of the reasons modern evangelicalism feels so thin is because it is merely modern; there is no connection with the thousands of years of saints who have gone before." But we need them; we need their fellowship and counsel, from their writings. You see how much I lean upon the Scottish poet George MacDonald; he is one of my companions. Who will be yours?

TO CLARIFY

If you haven't the foggiest idea where to begin to draw on the wisdom of the saints down through the ages, let me recommend Richard Foster's *Devotional Classics*, a wonderful compilation of many gems from many ages and authors.

WHO BEARS THE BURDEN?

"When I consider all that is at stake in this journey I am on, how vulnerable are my heart and the hearts of those I love, how quickly I forget, I am moved to fall on my face and cry out to God for the grace to remember." Are you feeling, as I often have, the pressure to keep all this going in your life?

How did you come by the Sacred Romance in the first place? Did you just sort of make all this up in your life?

But thank God, "the final burden of remembrance does not rest on us; if it did, we should all despair." On whom then does the burden rest? What does this allow your heart to do?

TO CLARIFY

In Philippians 1:6, Paul reminded us of a truth that truly lets our hearts rest:

> He who began a good work in you will carry it on to completion until the day of Christ Jesus (NIV).

> And I am certain that God, who began the good work within you, will continue his work until it is finally finished on the day when Christ Jesus returns (NLT).

> There has never been the slightest doubt in my mind that the God who started this great work in you would keep at it and bring it to a flourishing finish on the very day Christ Jesus appears (MSG).

REMINDERS ALONG THE WAY

"The Sacred Romance calls to us every moment of our lives. It whispers to us on the wind, invites us through the laughter of good friends, reaches out to us through the touch of someone we love. We've heard it in our favorite music, sensed it at the birth of our first child, been drawn to it while watching the shimmer of a sunset on the ocean. It is even present in times of great personal suffering—the illness of a child, the loss of a marriage, the death of a friend. Something calls to us through experiences like these and rouses an inconsolable longing deep within our heart, waking in us a yearning for intimacy, beauty, and adventure."

All we must do is keep an open heart and an open eye and ear, for our Lover is pursuing us still, will pursue us till the end of all time.

And then the real adventure begins.

WINDOWS

Film

Henry V (Fox, 1989). There are many versions of this wonderful story on film, but the best by far is this one, directed by and starring Kenneth Branagh.

Music

Legends of the Fall motion picture soundtrack (Sony Music, 1994). Track 2 is deeply moving.

"Joy in the Journey," title track from *Joy in the Journey* by Michael Card (Sparrow Records, 1994).

"Bright Side of the Road" by Van Morrison, from the *Best of Van Morrison* (Polydor Records, 1990).

Books

Devotional Classics, edited by Richard Foster and James Bryan Smith (San Francisco: HarperSanFrancisco, 1993).

The Journey of Desire by John Eldredge (Nashville, TN: Nelson Books, 2016). In many ways, it picks up where we've left off here and continues the Journey.

NOTES

1. G. K. Chesterton (1874–1936), "On Certain Modern Writers and the Institution of the Family," *Heretics* (London, UK: John Lane: The Bodley Head, 1905).

2. Ken Gire, *Windows of the Soul* (Grand Rapids, MI: Zondervan, 2017)

3. A. W. Tozer (1897–1963), *The Pursuit of God* (Reynoldsburg, OH: Christian Publications, Inc., 1948).

4. Gerald May (1940–2005), *Addiction and Grace* (New York: Harper & Row, 1967).

5. Augustine (354–430), *Homily 4 on the First Epistle of John*, from H. Browne, translator, *Nicene and Post-Nicene Father*, volume 7 (Buffalo, NY: Christian Literature Publishing Co., 1988).

6. C. S. Lewis (1898–1963), *The Weight of Glory* (London: Geoffrey Bles Publishers, 1949).

7. Matthew Arnold (1822–1888), "The Buried Life," written in 1852, published in *Matthew Arnold's Poetical Works* (New York: Thomas Y. Crowell & Co, 1897).

8. Frederick Buechner (1926–2022), *Telling Secrets* (San Francisco: HarperSanFrancisco, 1991).

9. Madame Guyon (1648–1717), cited in Thomas C. Upham, *The Life of Madame Guyon* (New York: Harper & Brothers, Publishers, 1847).

10. Annie Dillard, *Pilgrim at Tinker Creek* (New York: Harper and Row, 1974).

11. Buechner, *Now and Then: A Memoir of Vocation* (San Francisco: HarperSanFrancisco, 1983), emphasis added.

12. George MacDonald (1824–1905), "Abba, Father!", *Unspoken Sermons*, second series (London: Longmans, Green & Co., 1885).

13. MacDonald, *Diary of an Old Soul* (self-published, 1880).

14. Lewis, *The Problem of Pain* (London: The Centenary Press, 1940).

15. George Herbert (1593–1633), "*Jacula Prudentum*; or, *Outlandish Proverbs, Sentences, Etc.*," *The Canterbury Poets* (London: Walter Scott, Ltd., 1885).

16. Henry Wadsworth Longfellow (1807–1882), *Hyperion: A Romance*, volume 2 (New York: Samuel Colman, 1839).

17. Chesterton, "On Certain Modern Writers and the Institution of the Family," *Heretics*, 1905.

18. William Shakespeare (1564–1616), *Macbeth*, act v, scene v.

19. Chesterton, *Orthodoxy* (New York: John Lane Company, 1908).

20. Dallas Willard (1935–2013), *The Divine Conspiracy* (San Francisco: HarperOne, 1998).

21. Tozer, *The Knowledge of the Holy* (New York: Harper & Brothers, 1961).

22. Carl Jung (1875–1961), *The Development of Personality*, volume 17 in *The Collected Works of C. G. Jung* (London: Routledge Kegan Paul, 1953–1980), originally written 1910.

23. Daniel Taylor, *The Healing Power of Stories* (New York: Doubleday, 1996).

24. Robert McKee, *Story* (New York: ReganBooks, 1997).

25. C. John Sommerville, *How the News Makes Us Dumb* (Downer's Grove, IL: InterVarsity Press, 1999).

26. Shakespeare, *As You Like It*, act ii, scene vii.

27. Buechner, *Telling the Truth* (New York: Harper & Row, 1977).

28. Adapted from Walter Brueggemann, *A Commentary on Jeremiah* (Grand Rapids, MI: William B. Eerdmans Publishing Company, 1998). The exact quote reads, "To judge Jeremiah to be true is a theological verdict which allows for something wild, dangerous, unfettered, and free in the character of Yahweh."

29. Harold S. Kushner (1935–2023), *When Bad Things Happen to Good People* (New York: Schocken Books, 1981).

30. MacDonald, "Consuming Fire," *Unspoken Sermons*.

31. Chesterton, "On Certain Modern Writers and the Institution of the Family," *Heretics*.

32. Simon Tugwell, *Prayer: Living with God* (Springfield, IL: Templegate Publishing, 1975).

33. Herman Melville (1819–1891), "Letter to Nathaniel Hawthorne," June 1, 1851.

34. This letter was published in Lyle W. Dorsett and Marjorie Lamp Mead, editors, *C. S. Lewis: Letters to Children* (New York: Scribner, 1996).

35. Eugene Peterson (1932–2018), cited in Michael J. Cusick, "A Conversation with Eugene Peterson," *Mars Hill Review*, volume 3, issue 3, Fall 1995.

36. Lewis, *The Screwtape Letters* (London: Geoffrey Bles Publishers, 1942).

37. MacDonald, "Gloriously Wasteful, O My Lord, Art Thou," published in *A Book of Strife in the Form of the Diary of an Old Soul* (self-published, 1880).

38. Tozer, *The Pursuit of God*.

39. Philip Yancey, *Disappointment with God* (Grand Rapids: Zondervan, 1988).

40. Buechner, *Telling Secrets*.

41. Neil T. Anderson, *Victory Over the Darkness* (Ventura, CA: Regal Books, 1997).

42. T. S. Eliot (1888–1965), *The Rock* (New York: Harcourt, Brace and Company, 1934).

43. Stephen E. Ambrose (1936–2002), *D-Day* (New York: Simon & Schuster, 1994).

44. I suggest an approach to spiritual freedom developed by Neil Anderson called "The Seven Steps to Freedom in Christ." It's a series of questions and prayers that allow you to clean out the closets of your life and take away any opportunity the enemy might have found to oppress you. Many, many people have found a new level of freedom and release through this process. You can find the steps at the back of many of Anderson's books, including *The Bondage Breaker* (Eugene, OR: Harvest House Publishers, 2000/2019) and *Living Free in Christ* (Ventura, CA: Regal Books, 1993). Or visit his website at www.ficm.org.

45. Aristotle (384–322 bc), *Politics*, translated by Benjamin Jowett (Minneola, NY: Dover Publications, 2000).

46. May, *Addiction and Grace*.

47. MacDonald, *Diary of an Old Soul*.

48. John Donne (1572–1631), "Batter My Heart," *Holy Sonnets*, written 1609–1611.

49. MacDonald, *Diary of an Old Soul*.

50. Oswald Chambers (1874–1917), *My Utmost for His Highest* (New York: Dodd, Mead, & Co., 1935).

51. Lewis, *The Weight of Glory*.

52. Augustine, cited in Emilie Zum Brun, *St. Augustine: Being and Nothingness* (St. Paul, MN: Paragon House, 1988).

53. Guyon, cited in *Union with God* (Augusta, ME: Christian Books, 1981).

54. Willard, *The Spirit of the Disciplines* (San Francisco: HarperSanFrancisco, 1988).

55. Lewis, *The Weight of Glory*.

56. A. J. Conyers (1946–2004), *The Eclipse of Heaven* (Sound Bend, IN: St. Augustine Press, 1999).

57. Peter Kreeft, *Everything You Wanted to Know About Heaven* (San Francisco: Ignatius Press, 1990).

58. Lewis, *The Weight of Glory*.

59. MacDonald, cited in *The Heart of George MacDonald*, edited by Rolland Hein (New York: Doubleday, 2000).

60. J. R. R. Tolkien (1892–1973), *The Fellowship of the Ring* (London: Allen & Unwin, 1954).

61. John Bunyan (1628–1688), *The Pilgrim's Progress*, first published in 1678.

62. A great example and riveting book is *The Paradise King: The Tragic History and Spectacular Future of Everything According to Jesus of Nazareth*, by Blaine Eldredge (2023).

ABOUT THE AUTHOR

John Eldredge is a bestselling author and counselor. His numerous books include *Wild at Heart*, *Captivating* (with his wife, Stasi), *All Things New*, *Get Your Life Back*, and *Resilient*. He is also president of Wild at Heart, a ministry devoted to helping people discover the heart of God and recover their own hearts in God's love. John and his wife, Stasi, live near Colorado Springs, Colorado. To learn more, visit wildatheart.org.

JOHN ELDREDGE

WILD AT HEART
PODCAST

Wild at Heart offers weekly podcast
conversations with John Eldredge
and his team. It's free. It's powerful.
And it's better when you're in the
conversation with us.

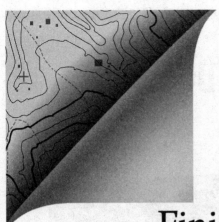

Finishing this study is only the beginning.

Continue your journey at
WildAtHeart.org

Weekly Podcasts

Video & Audio Resources

Prayers We Pray

Live Events

ALSO AVAILABLE FROM
JOHN ELDREDGE

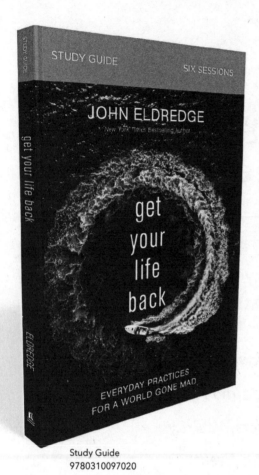

Study Guide
9780310097020

DVD
9780310097037

Available now at your favorite bookstore,
or streaming video on StudyGateway.com

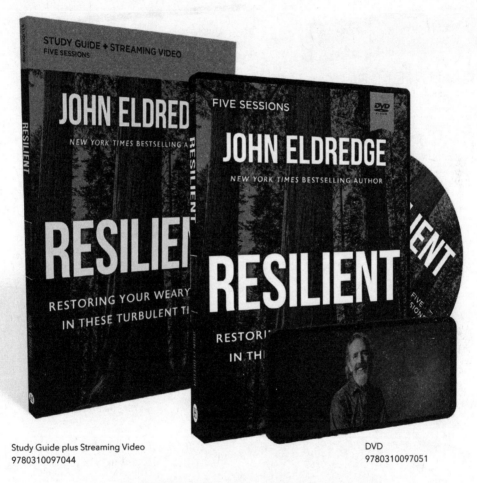

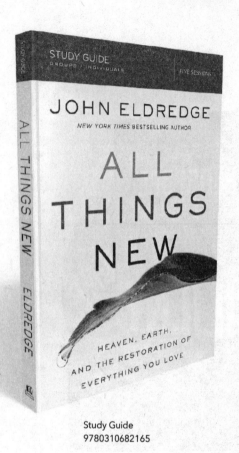

ALSO AVAILABLE FROM
JOHN ELDREDGE

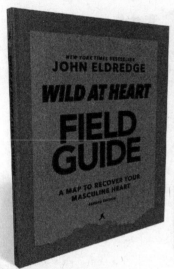

Field Guide
9780310135647

Study Guide
9780310129103

DVD + Streaming Access
9780310129127

Available now at your favorite bookstore,
or streaming video on StudyGateway.com

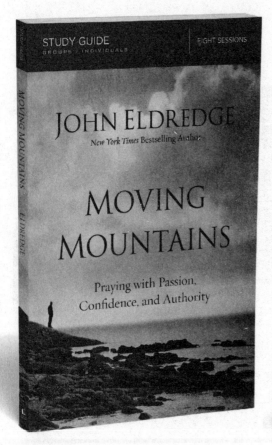
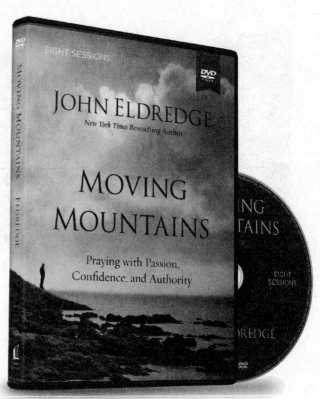

From the Publisher

GREAT STUDIES

ARE EVEN BETTER WHEN THEY'RE SHARED!

Help others find this study:

- Post a review at your favorite online bookseller.

- Post a picture on a social media account and share why you enjoyed it.

- Send a note to a friend who would also love it—or, better yet, go through it with them!

Thanks for helping others grow their faith!